all about POCKETS

storytime activities for early childhood

by Christine Petrell Kallevig

cover photograph by Eric Skarl
featuring an illustration by Jayme Wilkinson

International
P. O. Box 470505, Broadview Heights, Ohio 44147

Storytime Ink International
P. O. Box 470505, Broadview Heights, Ohio 44147

ISBN 0-9628769-6-8

Diagrams, patterns, and cover design by Christine Petrell Kallevig.
Cover photograph by Eric Skarl.
Illustration on page 61 by Jayme Wilkinson.

First Edition
10 9 8 7 6 5 4 3 2 1
Printed in the United States of America

Library of Congress Catalog Card Number: 93-083415

ACKNOWLEDGMENTS:
Every effort has been made to trace the ownership of all material and to secure the necessary permissions to reprint these selections. In the event of any questions arising as to the use of any material, the author and publisher, while expressing regret for any inadvertent error, will be happy to make the necessary correction in future printings.

Grateful acknowledgment is made to the following for permission to reprint the copyrighted material listed below:

Dover Publications, Inc. for "The Mice", "The Squirrel" and "The Bee Hive" by Emilie Poulsson from *Finger Plays For Nursery and Kindergarten*. Copyright © 1971 by Dover Publication, Inc.

Wilkinson, Jayme for illustration of mother with hand stuck in a child's pocket. Copyright © 1992 by Jayme Wilkinson.

The author expresses appreciation to...

The cordial and knowledgeable librarians on staff at the Cuyahoga County Public Library and the Akron - Summit County Library, for their invaluable assistance in researching this book.

Eric Skarl, for his sensitive photography skills.

Carol Clancy, for her astute editing and careful proof-reading.

Jayme Wilkinson, for his ability to capture energy and humor in his illustrations.

The talented storytellers of WRAPPS (Western Reserve Association for the Preservation and Perpetuation of Storytelling), for their generous contribution of ideas and resources. Special thanks to Jan Smuda, Pat Suchy, Nancy Wares, Ellen McConnell, and Deborah Hercsek.

Mary Jo Huff, for her unlimited creative energy and inspiring support.

To pocket lovers everywhere: It is an act of true love and faith when we open our pockets to reveal our secrets, our necessities, our treasures... May our pockets always hold something worth sharing. CPK

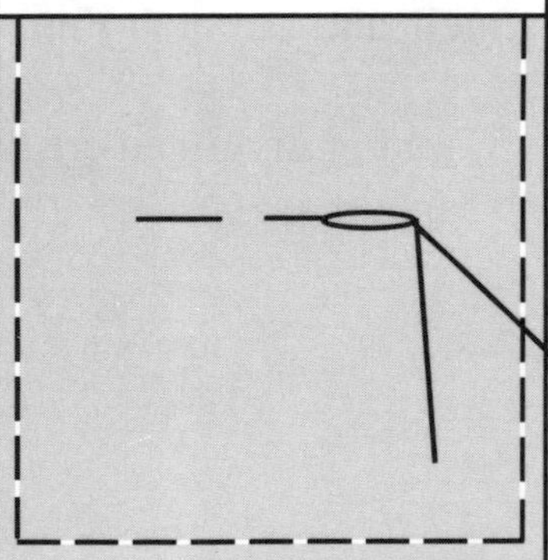

Contents

All about...
POCKETS?

Pockets are one thing, and hopefully not the *only* thing, that all people on Earth have in common.

Everyone wears pockets.

Everyone enjoys pockets.

Young children love pockets just as much as adults do.

Pockets unify generations.

Everyone has carried something in a pocket that really didn't belong in one... and loves to tell all about it.

We all lose things out of pocket holes.

We all whisper, "I have something in my pocket, and you can't guess it...."

None of us can resist thinking about what that *something* must be.

Yes, we all have pockets, love pockets, are curious about pockets, tell stories about pockets.... But it hasn't always been that way. Many years ago, we used to carry our secrets in bags. But since these ancient bags were called pockets, perhaps it wasn't so different after all....

Did you know that...

The word pocket comes to English from the French word poquette or poque (which are also roots to the similar words poach and pouch), meaning a small bag, or to poke. The earliest reference to the word *pocket* is found in 1280, when "pochetto" described a small bag or pouch used for carrying or as a means of measurement. "Three and twenty blackbirds, a *pocketful* of rye... " refers to a specific measurement, rather than to someone carrying a handful of grain in their pants.

Small bags have been found in every part of the world, and were probably among the first inventions. As cultures advanced, decoration became a part of bag making, and in many places, bags became status symbols. By 1430, a reference to "pockettis" was made, where the small bag was actually worn on the person, first tucked into a man's codpiece, an ornamented bag or flap attached to the front of the tight breeches of the 15th and 16th centuries. The codpiece, which at first formed an opening, or fly, to the trousers, finally became unfashionable when its exaggerated size became ridiculous and unmanageable.

The bag then was drawn up at the top (the drawstring pocket described on page 119) and dangled from a man's waist. Women tied their pockets to their waists and hid them under their skirts until the 1830's, except for a brief period in the early 1800's when the popularity of sheer cotton dresses made hidden pockets impossible.

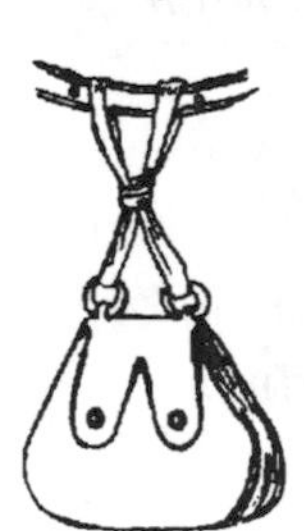

The first pockets that were actually sewn permanently into men's trousers appeared near the end of the 16th century. These first pockets began when an opening was made in the side seams of the tight fitting trousers of the 1500's so that a man could insert a cloth pouch containing his belongings. The independent pouch soon became a sewn-in feature as seen in this 1570 quote from Fox, "He bare alwayes about hym, in hys bosome or pocket, a litle booke contayning the Psalmes of David."

The idea of a pocketbook was introduced in 1510 by Aldus Manutius, an Italian publisher. These early books were small enough to be carried in pockets, and usually contained religious text, mathematical tables, or other useful information. Later, blank pages were added so that merchants could write important notes, the origin of the modern notebook.

In the late 17th century, the pocketbook took on a new role.

Bankers began printing forms promising a certain amount of gold (paper money). People didn't want to carry these important papers in a pouch or wallet, so they were hidden between the pages of a pocketbook. Soon, a craftsman developed a new money holder similar to a pocketbook, but without pages. Eventually, all connections to books were eliminated, but the name, pocketbook, and its relationship to money, remain.

By the 1600's, pockets became a standard design feature of men's and women's capes and coats, at first located at the hem of an overcoat, and then eventually moving up to the hip. By 1700, coats had pockets with flaps and scalloped edges positioned at hip level. 18th century dresses still did not have pockets sewn into them. Pockets were small bags sewn onto a ribbon and tied around the waist, hence "Lucy Locket lost her pocket...." They were reached through a slit in the skirt.

Pockets were modified and given great importance by Levi Strauss, the tailor responsible for designing and popularizing blue jeans. Miners complained that the weight of tools caused pockets to split at the seams, so in 1873, Strauss solved the problem by applying copper rivets at the seams. Pocket rivets were finally abandoned in 1937 when school principals complained that back pocket rivets were scratching and damaging wooden desks and benches beyond repair.

The need to keep track of car keys has given pockets increasing importance for 20th century men and women, so that now almost every modern garment contains a pocket. And that brings us back to the convenience and fun of a book all about pockets...

You've probably guessed by now that...

All the activities in this book have something to do with pockets, either in the way they are presented or in their actual subject matter. Hopefully, the methods and suggestions for extending and applying the activities will serve as a launching pad for further ideas. All of the stories, songs, poems, and games emphasize an active, hands-on, physical learning style that is most effective in the early childhood years. All of them make use of the important eye-ear-hand-body-movement connectedness that defines the cognitive ability of young children.

The early stages of critical thinking and emotional responsiveness are also included. These elements are woven into the extended activities, to be applied according to the unique characteristics and needs of particular groups and settings.

Yes, you do need to wear a pocket when you use this book... Regular old pants pockets are fine, overalls are better, and storytelling aprons are best of all. Patterns and directions for making pockets are included, as well as complete instructions for pocket crafts and illustrations for flannel board characters. Annotated bibliographies listing other sources related to pocket poems, stories, and pouched animals can be found at the end of each section.

So, now all we have to do is follow the advice of poet Beatrice Schenk de Regniers: "Keep a poem in your pocket and a picture in your head, and you'll never feel lonely at night when you're in bed...." The good news is, when we share our pocket poems, those around us won't be lonely either!

Resources for pocket history:

Bell, Quentin, *On Human Finery*, 1976, Schocken Books, New York, NY.

Funk, Wilfred, *Word Origins and their Romantic Stories*, 1950, Funk & Wagnalls, New York, NY.

Panati, Charles, *Extraordinary Origins of Everyday Things,* 1987, Harper & Row, Publishers, Inc. New York, NY.

Perl, Lila, *From Top Hats to Baseball Caps, From Bustles to Blue Jeans: Why We Dress the Way We Do*, 1990, Clarion Books, New York, NY.

Tortora, Phyllis & Eubank, Keith, *A Survey of Historic Costume,* 1989, Fairchild Publications, New York.

Vanoni, Marvin, *Great Expressions: How Our Favorite Words and Phrases Have Come to Mean What They Mean*, 1989, William Morrow and Co., Inc., New York, NY.

Poems and Rhymes for
Pocket Play

Put A Secret In Your Pocket

Put a secret in your pocket
and a smile on your face,
and you'll always have a friend
in each and every place.

The secret warms your smile,
and brings you secret fun.
The pocket keeps your secret
as warmly as the sun.

So put a secret in your pocket
and a smile on your face,
and you'll always have a friend
in each and every place.

Christine Petrell Kallevig

"You will never be alone with a poet in your pocket."
Letter to John Quincy Adams, May 12, 1780

Rhymes emphasizing finger and hand coordination

The rhythm in these action rhymes promotes smooth and natural movements while stimulating both auditory and visual skills.

My Fingers - CPK

I have ten fingers.
They stand tall,
Wave hello,
Make a ball.
They push buttons
For a call.

I have ten fingers.
They shake hands,
Wave bye-bye,
Stretch rubber bands.
They march like legs,
Do handstands.

I have ten fingers.
They do it all.
Tie, button, clap,
Catch a ball.
Open, shut, turn,
Stop a fall.

I have ten fingers.
They fill my pockets
With stuff I want,
Like planes and rockets,
Pennies, suckers,
Golden lockets.

I have ten fingers.
Watch them swarm!
I think I'll keep them
Snug and warm
In my pockets,
Safe from harm.

Options:

1. Before you begin, ask the children to join in by reciting the line, "I have ten fingers" each time you say it. Ask them to listen carefully and watch so that they can make their fingers do the actions along with you. Pause with each motion to give them enough time to model you.
2. Try the rhyme a second time without saying the words, except for the children chanting, "I have ten fingers." The children must watch carefully to follow the actions. Point to them when it's their turn to chant the repeating phrase.
3. Ask, "What do your fingers do?" When a child tells you, ask them to stand and show you. Then ask the whole group to make their fingers act it out too. Some new ideas might be: paint, draw, color, stir, snap, build, dig, plant, carry.

Ten Fingers - anonymous

I have ten little fingers
And they belong to me.
I can make them do things.
Would you like to see?
I can shut them up tight,
Or open them wide.
I can put them together or make them all hide.
I can make them jump high.
I can make them jump low.
I can fold them quietly
And hold them just so.

Options:

1. Make the motions suggested in the rhyme. Put your hands in your pockets to "make them hide."
2. Repeat a second time with the children joining in, substituting "we" for "I", and "us" for "me". This is a good way to settle a group for stories.

This Is The Circle That Is My Head

a variation of a traditional rhyme

This is the circle that is my head.
This is my mouth where words are said.
These are my eyes with which I see.
This is my nose that's a part of me.
This is my pocket for all things found
Like secrets and treasures all around!

Options:

1. Ask, "What treasures have you put in your pockets?" or "Have you ever put something in your pocket that you didn't want anyone else to know about? This is a secret thing."
2. This rhyme makes a good lead-in to the poem "Put A Secret In Your Pocket" (p. 11), the story, "Not Rubber Bands" (p. 37), and several picture storybooks with themes of discovering treasures: *Peter's Pocket, David's Pocket* and *Peter's Pockets* (sources on p. 47-50).

My Hands - variation of traditional rhyme
My hands upon my head I place,
On my shoulders, on my face;
In my pockets I put them so,
All my fingers in a row.
Now I raise them up so high,
Make my fingers dance and fly.
Now I clap them, one, two, three,
Then I fold them silently.

Options:

1. Encourage the children to do the motions with you the first time through. The second time through, omit the underlined words, encouraging the children to say them. On the third try, everyone omits the underlined words and only does the actions, whispering the last line so that the word *silently* is merely mouthed.
2. Try striking a rhythm instrument one time, only on the underlined words. Take out two rhythm instruments and ask two children to come up and help you. Give them the instruments and ask them to play only on the word *head*. Praise them when they do it correctly, then ask two others to come up for *shoulders* and the other key words until each child has had a chance. Next, give each child an instrument, and try the activity as a group. Have them put all the instruments down on the last line. Collect them or go on to another musical activity.

?

When is a pocket like two letters of the alphabet?
When it's M T!

How can your pocket be empty and still have something in it?
It can have a hole in it!

What side of the pocket is most empty?
The outside!

A Pocket - CPK

A pocket is a good thing to be.
It carries things needed by me.
A quarter, a dime,
A tissue, a key,
Each one a necessity.

Options:

1. As you recite the rhyme, pull each of the objects from your pocket. Then start the rhyme again. When you get to the third line, ask children to volunteer objects from their pockets and substitute them. In the unlikely event that no one has anything in their pockets, have a second pocket of yours loaded and ready to show. Then say, "Think of some things that you need during the day. Pretend they are in your pocket." Then start the rhyme again, naming imaginary necessities.
2. This rhyme makes a good lead-in to the stories, "The Pocket Holes of Pocketville" (p. 43) and "Penny's Paper Pocket" (p. 40).

Right Hand, Left Hand - variation of traditional rhyme

This is my right hand.
I'll raise it up high.
This is my left hand.
I'll touch the sky.
Right hand, left hand,
Roll them around.
Left hand, right hand,
Pound, pound, pound.

This is my right pocket.
I'll pull something out.
This is my left pocket.
I'll toss it about.
Right pocket, left pocket,
Close them like that.
Left pocket, right pocket,
Pat, pat, pat.

Options:

1. Mirror the actions or turn your back to the group so that they are modeling the correct right and left hands as you do the motions suggested by the rhyme.
2. Ask, "What do you think I pretended to pull out of my pocket?" Wait for answers, then pretend to pull out tiny things like paper clips or marbles, medium things like balls or cookies, large things like books or shoes, and then improbable huge things like elephants or trees. Ask, "What do you think would really fit in my pocket?" This is a good lead-in to the game, "Pocket Charades" on page 68.

Sleepy Fingers - anonymous

Hold your hand in front of your pocket and slip your fingers in, one at a time, starting with the smallest finger and ending with the thumb.

My fingers are so sleepy;
It's time they went to bed.
So first you, Baby Finger,
Tuck in your little head.

Ring man, now it's your turn,
And next, Tall Man great.
Now, Pointer Finger, hurry!
Because it's getting late.

Let's see if all are snuggled.
No, here's one more to come.
Move over, everyone.
Make room for Mister Thumb.

Options:

1. Inserting fingers one at a time is difficult for most young children, so give them plenty of time or allow them to use their spare hand to help put in the finger.
2. Sing "Busy Fingers" (p. 54) and "Where is Thumpkin?" (p. 56).
3. Read *Joey* by Jack Kent (source on page 97), where mother kangaroo finally does run out of space.

What time is it when an elephant climbs into your pocket?
Time to get a bigger pocket!

Why is an empty pocket always the same?
Because there's no change in it!

Hands on Shoulders - CPK

Hands on shoulders, hands on knees,
Hands in pockets, if you please.
Touch your chin, now your nose,
Now your ears and now your toes.
Hands up high, like a tree,
Clap them loudly, one, two, three!

Options:

1. Recite slowly the first time, then a little faster, and then very fast. This rhyme makes a good stretching exercise after a long sitting period, but be prepared for giggles! It can be used either sitting or standing.
2. Add "Simon says" to parts of this rhyme: "Simon says hands on shoulders, Simon says hands on knees, Simon says hands in pockets, if you please." Then leave it out of other parts. Children do the actions only when they hear "Simon says". Try using another signal for doing the actions, such as the sound of a bell or rhythm instrument. Children do the actions only when they hear the bell.

Pockets - anonymous

There's something in my pocket.
Could it be a moose? *(Hands over head for antlers.)*
Could it be a train with a bell and a caboose?
(Elbows to side and move arms in a circle.)
Could it be a snake? *(Wiggle body.)*
Or some sticky icky glue? *(Open hands slowly.)*
Right here in my pocket is...
A KISS from me to you! *(Blow kiss.)*

Options:

1. Divide the children into three groups: the moose, cabooses, and snakes. Repeat the rhyme, giving each group time to act out their parts. Everyone does the motions for glue and kissing. Trade parts, so that all children have a chance to act out all the characters.
2. Ask, "If you were a pocket, what would you want in you? What type of clothing would you want to be attached to? Who would you like to wear you? What size of a pocket would you be? What color fabric would you like to be made from?" Draw pictures of their answers.

Rhymes emphasizing gross motor coordination

The rhymes in this section assist young children in discovering their body parts and what these parts can do in space in relation to others. Combining movement and imagination help to integrate the learning modalities while promoting teamwork and individual self concepts.

Stuff Your Pocket - CPK

Stuff your pocket,
Stuff your pocket,
Stuff it just like me.
Slip in a penny
And a tiny house key.

Stuff your pocket,
Stuff your pocket,
Stuff it just like me.
Put in a pebble
And a little green pea.

Stuff your pocket,
Stuff your pocket,
Stuff it just like me.
Pour in some honey
For a little buzzing bee.
AH OH...OUCH!

Options:

1. This poem works well with real or imaginary props.
2. The rhythm of this verse is perfect for teaching clapping patterns. Start with individuals simply clapping together as a group, then try an alternating knees-clap pattern, then try clapping patterns with partners according to the sequence shown on the next page.
3. When teaching new clapping patterns with partners, start by slowly repeating the directions, "Clap together, knees, clap together, knees...", only gradually picking up speed. When the children know the clapping pattern and are demonstrating it successfully, then introduce the rhyme. Never introduce more than one or two new patterns a day and always start the day with an easy pattern that your children already know. Many songs and nursery rhymes are appropriate to accompany clapping patterns, but be sure that the verses have a regular beat. All of the clapping patterns for young children should be in 4/4 time. It is always fun to see how many rhymes the teacher can recite in the background before the children lose the pattern. See page 32 for more rhymes.

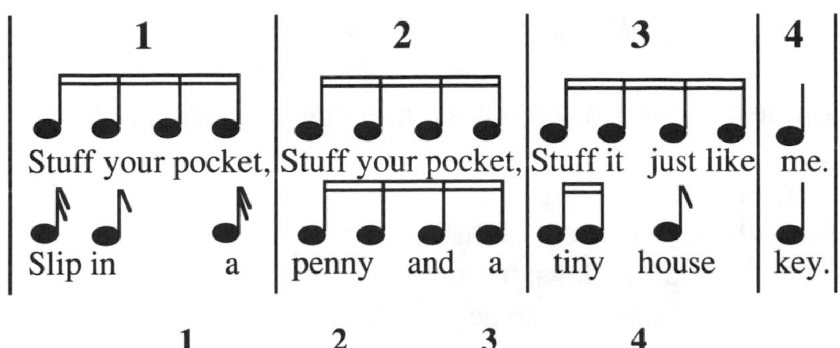

	1	2	3	4
1.	clap-T	clap-T	clap-T	clap-T
2.	clap-T	knees	clap-T	knees
3.	clap-T	clap-A	clap-T	clap-A
4.	clap-A	clap-A	knees	knees
5.	clap-T	clap-T	knees	knees
6.	clap-T	clap-T	clap-A	clap-A
7.	clap-T1	clap-T1	clap-T1	clap-T1
8.	*same as #7, only switch hands to other side, mirroring each other*			
9.	*same as #7, only alternate hands, mirroring each other*			
10.	clap-R	clap-R	clap-R	clap-R
11.	clap-L	clap-L	clap-L	clap-L
12.	clap-R	clap-R	clap-L	clap-L
13.	clap-R	clap-L	clap-R	clap-L
14.	clap-R	clap-L	clap-T	clap-T
15.	clap-R	clap-L	clap-T	knees

clap-T = clap both hands together with both hands of your partner.

clap-A = clap alone, or clap your own hands together.

clap-T1 = clap one hand together with partner's one hand on the same side.

clap-R = clap right hands only, crossing the midline.

clap-L = clap left hands only, crossing the midline.

Making Friends - anonymous

A little boy lived in this house. *(Point to your right pocket.)*
A little girl lived in this house.
(Point to your left pocket, then slip hands in the pockets.)
The little boy came out of his house. *(Pull the right hand out.)*
He looked up and down the street.
He didn't see any one, so he went back into his house.
(Put the right hand back in.)
The little girl came out of her house. *(Pull the left hand out.)*
She looked up and down the street.
She didn't see anyone, so she went back into her house.
(Put the left hand back in.)
The next day, the little boy came out of his house and looked all around. *(Right hand out.)*
The little girl came out of her house and looked all around.
(Left hand out.)
They saw each other.
They walked across the street and shook hands. *(Shake hands.)*
Then the little boy went back into his house. *(Right hand in.)*
The little girl went back into her house. *(Left hand in.)*
Until they met again the next day.

Options:

1. After reciting the poem a couple times, ask the boys to form a line and the girls to form another across from them. They each step forward one step when they "come out of the house" and step one step backward when they go back in. They act out the rest of the motions (looking around, shaking hands) and sit down at the very end.
2. Instead of forming lines, ask the boys to stand up and quickly sit down whenever they hear the word, *boy;* girls will do the same whenever they hear the word, *girl*. If your group gets too stimulated and silly, ask them to raise and lower their hands instead of standing up.
3. Ask, "Has anyone made a new friend lately? How do you meet new friends? What do you say?" Use this rhyme to lead into stories about making new friends.
4. Read *Little New Kangaroo*, by Bernard Wiseman (source on page 99). It is about meeting new friends.

The Mice - adapted from a poem by Emilie Poulsson

Five little mice on the kitchen floor,
(Five fingers of one hand scurry on the floor.)
Seeking bread crumbs or something more.
Five little mice on the shelf up high,
(Five fingers of the other hand scurry up high.)
Feasting so daintily on a pie.
But the big round eyes of the wise old cat
(Make circles around your eyes.)
See what the five little mice are at.
Quickly she jumps! but the mice run away,
(Stuff both hands quickly into your pockets.)
And hide in their snug little holes all day.
Feasting in kitchens may be very nice;
"But home is the best!" say the five little mice.

Options:

1. Repeat the poem so that the children can recite the words and model the actions with you.
2. Ask, "What else might the mice enjoy eating?" Say the poem again, substituting the children's suggestions.
3. Spread out and act the poem out, emphasizing the gross motor activities of reaching, jumping, running, and crouching. If the motions are too stimulating for your group, break up into smaller groups, allowing only one group to act out the words at a time while the others stay seated, reciting the words with the regular actions.
4. Read *Two In A Pocket* by Robin Ravilious (source p. 49). It is about a mouse who is stalked by a cat until he finds a home in a pocket. Recite "Hickory Dickory Docket" (p. 34) and try the trick on p. 81. Several of the hamster activities on p. 83-88 would also work well with this rhyme.

?

What gets bigger, the more you take away?
A hole.

What runs around a pocket yet never moves?
An edge!

King of France - anonymous

The famous King of France,
He led ten thousand men.
He marched them way, way up the hill
And marched them down again.
And when they were up, they were up, up, up;
And when they were down, they were down, down, down;
And when they were only halfway up,
They were neither up nor down.

Options:

1. *Up* is above your head in the air. *Down* is touching the floor. Halfway is hands in your pocket. Ask the children to make their voices sound high on *up* and use low pitches on *down*.
2. Repeat with the children. This is a great stretching exercise after a long period of sitting still. It makes a good lead in to "Ten Little Soldiers".

Ten Little Soldiers - anonymous

Ten little soldiers standing in a row.
They all bow down to the captain, so.
They march to the left, they march to the right.
They all stand straight, quite ready to fight.
Along comes a little boy looking for some fun.
"Boo!" he shouts and laughs to see those soldiers run!

Options:

1. Use your fingers as soldiers, do the suggested motions, and let them run into your pockets at the end.
2. Repeat, but let the children say "Boo!"
3. Emphasize the right and left directions by turning around when saying that line.
4. Use this rhyme as a gross-motor activity on the playground or in a large movement room. Substitute the number of children in your group for "ten", or decide how many you'd like in each group. Groups of three or four are very manageable. Ask only one group to act out the motions at a time, while the others stay seated, reciting the words and taking the part of the boy who shouts "Boo!" Designate a particular place that they should run to in the end: chairs, a circle, next to a certain tree, etc.

Cobbler, Cobbler - variation of traditional rhyme

Cobbler, cobbler, mend my shoe *(point to shoe)*,
Have it done by half-past two *(hold up two fingers)*.
Stitch it up *(all stand up)*,
Stitch it down *(all sit down)*,
Nail the heel in all around *(pound the floor)*.

Tailor, tailor mend my pocket *(point to pocket)*,
Have it done like a rocket *(thrust arms up)*.
Stitch it up *(all stand up)*,
Stitch it down *(all sit down)*,
Sew the pocket all around *(stretch arms wide open)*.

Hatter, hatter mend my hat *(point to head)*,
Have it done, just like that (snap fingers).
Stitch it up *(all stand up)*,
Stitch it down *(all sit down)*,
Make it fit me like a crown *(make a point over head)*.

Hosier, hosier, mend my sock *(point to your socks)*,
Have it done by six o'clock *(hold up six fingers)*.
Stitch it up *(all stand up)*,
Stitch it down *(all sit down)*,
Darn the holes all around *(stretch arms wide open)*.

Options:

1. Recite with the appropriate actions. Repeat, but omit the underlined words, letting the children say them.
2. Try the rhyme with a pocketful of props (a shoe, a hat, a pocket, and a sock). Allow a child to come up and pick one out. The order of the verses would be determined by the prop selected. Let the children wear the props for the activity.
3. This is a good lead-in to the stories, "The Pocket Holes of Pocketville" (page 43) and "The Pocket Farm" (page 45). Make sewing cards or coloring papers from the illustrations on pages 24 and 25.

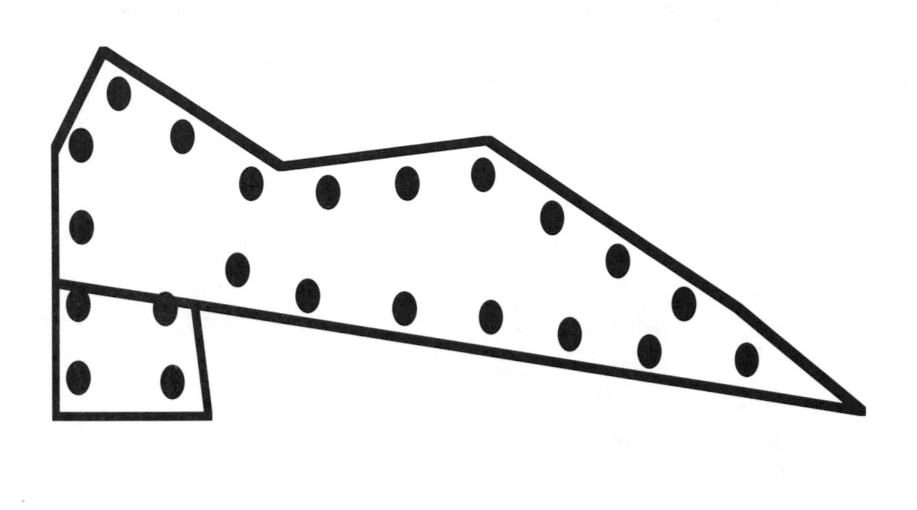

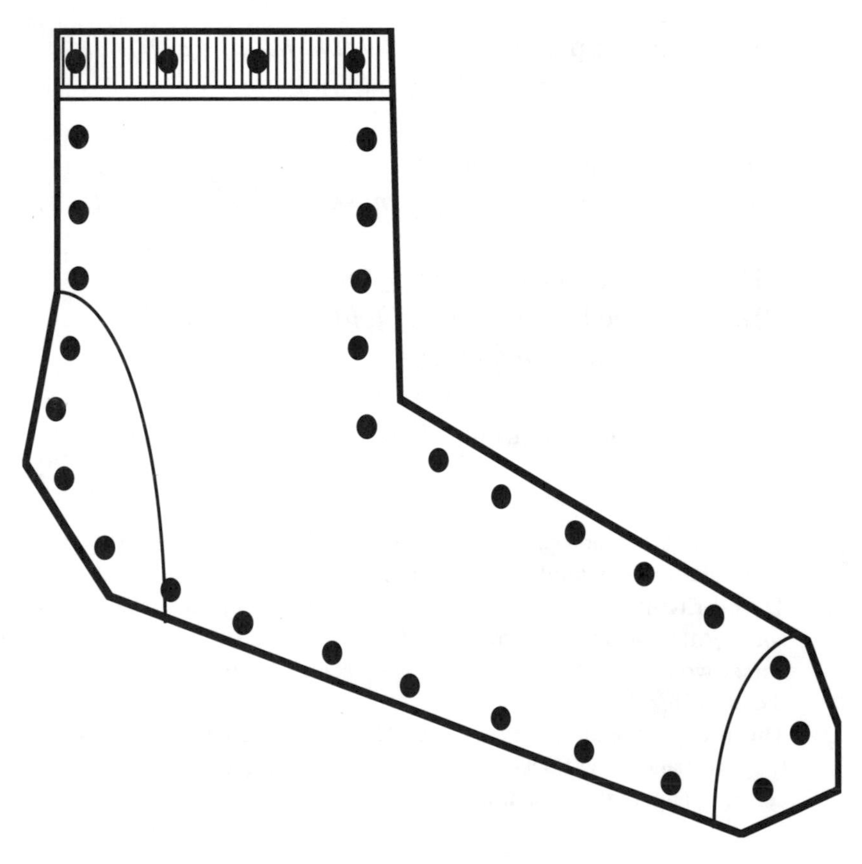

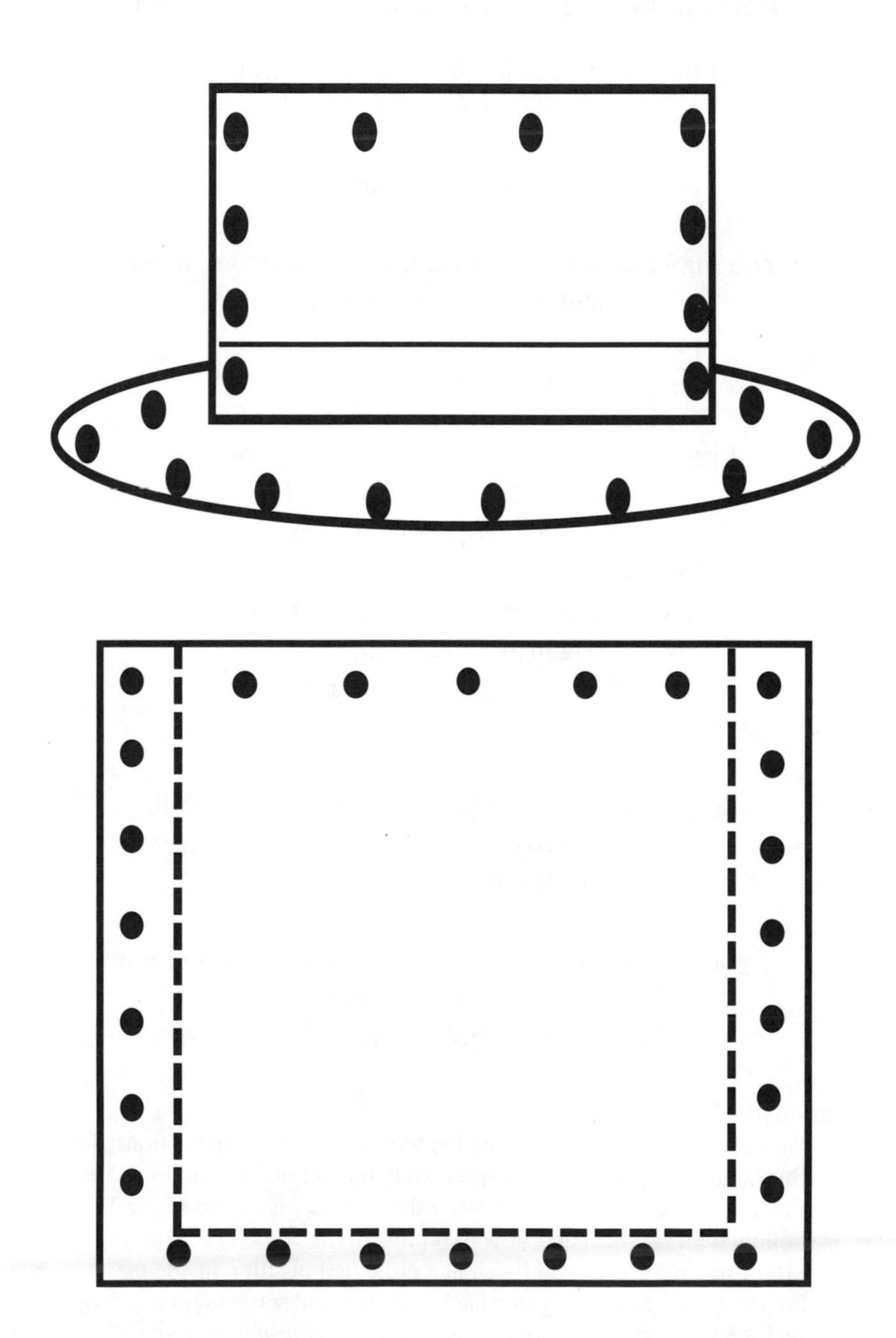

The Squirrel - adapted from a poem by Emilie Poulsson

Little squirrel, living there in the hollow tree,
(Make a large circle to represent the hollow tree.)
I've a pretty cage for you.
Come and live with me!

You may turn the little wheel, that will be great fun!
(Roll your hands around.)
Slowly round, or very fast,
If you faster run.

Little squirrel, I will bring, in my pocket here
Every day a feast of nuts!
Come, then, squirrel dear.

But the little squirrel said from his hollow tree,
(Large circle again.)
"Oh! no, no! I'd much rather
live here and be free!"

So my cage is empty yet, and the wheel is still;
But my little pocket here
Often with nuts, I fill.

If you like, I'll crack the nuts, some for you and me,
For the squirrel has enough
In his hollow tree.

Options:

1. Repeat while the children recite the words and model the actions. The third time, ask your group to spread out and act out the motions. Let them crouch on the floor in front of them to represent the squirrel's hollow tree, spin fast and slow to represent the wheel, hold out hands to offer imaginary nuts, and finish in a crouched position inside the hollow tree. Gather the group back together and settle them down by reciting the rhyme, "Warm Hands." *(options continue on page 27.)*

Warm Hands - anonymous
Warm hands, warm,
Do you know how?
If you want to warm your hands,
Warm your hands now.
(Stuff your hands into real or pretend pockets.)

Whirling Leaves - anonymous
The little leaves are whirling
Round, round, round.
The little leaves are whirling round
And falling to the ground.
Round, round, round, round,
(whisper)
Falling to the ground.

Leaves - CPK
The leaves drop from up high,
Yellow, brown, and red.
Floating gently from the sky,
Oops! One's on my head!

The leaves land where they will,
Yellow, red, and brown,
In the meadow, on the hill,
Oops! Deep in my pocket down.

What is quiet when alive, and noisy when dead?
A Leaf!

2. Recite, "Whirling Leaves" and then take out different colored leaves from your pocket. Use different colors of the same species (same shape, different colors) and same colors of different species (same color, different shape). Ask the children to identify all the ways they are alike and different. Sort them according to color, then shape (species).
3. Recite "Leaves." This rhyme makes an ideal lead-in to the story, "The Pocket Farm" on page 45.

Pocket Clocks - variation of a traditional rhyme

Great big clocks make a sound like
(Make big circle with arms overhead.)
T-i-c-k, t-o-c-k, t-i-c-k, t-o-c-k.
(Swing arms like a big pendulum.)
Medium clocks make a sound like
(Make a smaller circle with hands.)
Tick tock, tick tock, tick tock, tick tock.
(Swish the wrists back and forth quickly.)
And tiny little pocket clocks go
(Make a small circle with fingers.)
Ticket tocket, ticket tocket, ticket tocket, ticket tocket.
(Wag the index fingers back and forth.)
Back in the pocket!

Options:

1. Recite, "Hickory Dickory Docket" on page 34.
2. Bring a real pocket watch and demonstrate how it works. Let the children tell about the watches and clocks that they have in their families.
3. Show the movie "Alice In Wonderland", featuring the white rabbit's pocket watch.
4. Make pocket watches. Trace or copy the watch illustrated below. Attach string or yarn to the watch and pin it just inside the children's pockets for them to take home with them. Add movable watch hands for further practice with telling time.

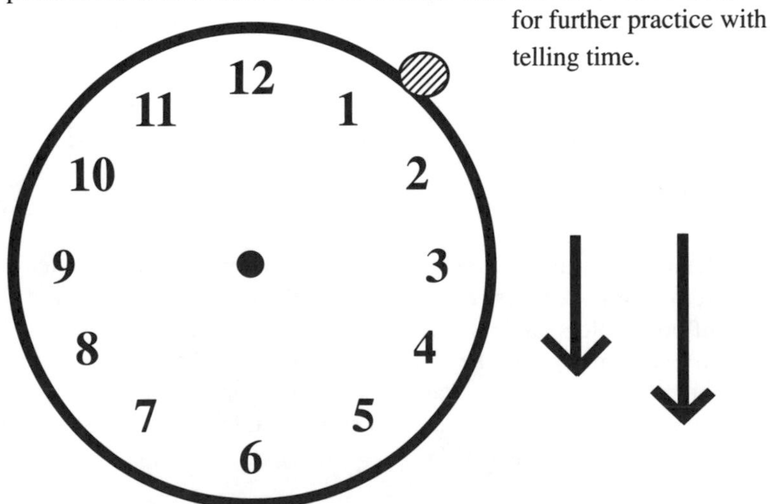

Counting Rhymes

Ten pocket aprons or multi-pocket boards (patterns on p. 115-121) are perfect props for these counting activities. Sing the song "Ten Little Pockets" on p. 57. Then count all the pockets in your group or room. Group each person according to the number of pockets he/she is wearing. Compare the groups. Then sort according to other attributes, such as color, size, fasteners, zippers, shape, decals, etc.

Ten Things - CPK

I have ten things in my pocket
Will you count them all for me?
First falls out a rabbit
And then some old candy.

Third, a wiggling snake
Zips out across the floor.
And then a buzzing bee
Darts out for number four.

Five and six are seesaw seats,
Pumping up and down.
Seven and eight are crabby geese,
Honking with a frown.

When we get to nine and ten,
Look around, see the grins.
For popping out of pocket now
Are big and wide hippo twins.

Go back in things! Back in the pocket now!
10-9-8-7-6-5-4-3-2-1...All done!

Options:

1. Use real or imaginary props. Be sure to hold up the proper number of fingers for each item.
2. Ask ten children to volunteer to act out the parts. Build a giant pocket by folding over a large quilt or blanket. Ask the volunteers to lie down under the cover and come out when it is their turn. The children pretending to be a seesaw can hold hands and take turns squatting and standing. The child pretending to be a piece of candy can roll or somersault out of the "pocket." Repeat so that everyone who wants a turn can get a turn. Your children will love you for taking a turn too.

Old Shoes, New Shoes - CPK

Old shoes, new shoes,
Black and brown and blue shoes,
One, two, three, four,
Tapping softly on the floor.

Old pants, new pants,
Black and brown and blue pants,
Five, six, seven, eight,
Tapping softly on the gate.

Old pockets, new pockets,
Black and brown and blue pockets,
eight, seven, six, five,
Tapping softly on the side.

Old shirts, new shirts,
Black and brown and blue shirts,
four, three, two, one,
Tapping softly just for fun.

Shoes, pants, pockets, shirts,
Up to eight, down to one,
Black and blue, old and new,
Now our tapping game is through.

Options:

1. *Motions:* Sway to the left on *old*, sway to the right on *new*. Point to the article of clothing on the second line. Hold up fingers as you count. Tap according to directions.
2. Use a flannel board to add and take away the numbers. Then give each child eight counters (beans, small blocks, clips, chips, etc.) and ask them to put down and take away the correct amount as you recite the poem.
3. Distribute rhythm instruments. Recite the poem as the children play their instruments on the particular piece of clothing: hold the drum (or sticks, triangle, etc.) on their shoes, then on their pants, pockets, shirts, and on all four places on the last verse.
4. Sing "We All Put Our Clothes On" on page 57.

Bee Hive - Emilie Poulsson

Begin with your hand in your
pocket to represent the bee hive.

Here is the bee hive.
Where are the bees?
Hidden away where nobody sees.
Soon they come creeping out of the hive -
(Bring out one finger at a time.)
One! - two! - three! - four! - five!

Five Little Ants - anonymous

Begin with your hand in your pocket
to represent the ant hill.

Five little ants in an ant hill,
Busily working and never still.
Do you think they're in there?
Do you think they're really alive?
See them come out,
(Bring out one finger at a time.)
One, two, three, four, five.

Five little ants near an ant hill,
Busily working and never still.
Look! They found some food
To keep them alive.
See them go in,
(Put in one finger at a time.)
One, two, three, four, five.

One, Two Buckle Your Shoe - traditional

(Pantomime the actions.)
One, two, buckle your shoe,
Three, four, shut the door,
Five, six, pick up sticks,
Seven, eight, lay them straight,
Nine, ten, a big fat hen *(Big circle with arms)*,
Eleven, twelve, who will delve?*
(One hand holding a magnifying glass, the other a book),
Thirteen, fourteen, girls a counting
(Finger points as though counting),
Fifteen, sixteen, girls a missing
(Hand on forehead on the lookout),
Seventeen, eighteen, girls a waiting *(Crossed arms)*,
Nineteen, twenty, oops! my pocket's empty.

*Define this word as someone who delves into the facts, or as someone who really wants to know something and asks questions or studies a lot.

Options:

1. Take counters out of a pocket as you say the rhymes, then have the group count them as you put them back in. Distribute portable pockets (p. 122) each containing up to 20 counters. Spread out and repeat the rhymes slowly as each child takes out a counter of their own, counting them again as a group as they put them back in the pockets.
2. Since you already have out the portable pockets, this is a good lead-in to the game, "Pocket Pass" on page 69.

When can a ball travel far, without being thrown, hit, or rolled?

When it's carried in a pocket!

***Pocketized* Nursery Rhymes and those already *Pocketed*...** Most of these rhymes make excellent accompaniment for ball bouncing, passing games, jumproping, partner clapping (see page 19), or other repetitive motions. For example, if you'd like to encourage your children to become more comfortable with crossing their midlines, simply take your left hand and cross it to your right shoulder as you recite a rhyme. Use the steady rhythm of the rhyme like background music. As the children say the rhyme and mimic your actions, they will internalize the rhythm and the steady beat. Other actions might be right hand to left ear, left hand to right knee, or crossing the hands together with the swinging motion of a pendulum.

Sing a Song of Sixpence - traditional nursery rhyme

Pocket here refers to a unit of measurement.

Sing a song of sixpence, a *pocket* full of rye,
Four and twenty blackbirds baked in a pie.
When the pie was opened,
The birds began to sing.
Wasn't that a dainty dish to set before a king!

The king was in his counting house,
Counting out his money.
The queen was in the parlor,
Eating bread and honey.
The maid was in the garden,
hanging out the clothes,
When down came a blackbird,
And nipped off her nose!

Lucy Locket - traditional nursery rhyme

Lucy Locket lost her pocket,
Kitty Fisher found it;
Not a penny was there in it,
Only ribbon round it.

Pocket here refers to the bag that was tied to a woman's waist and dangled beneath her skirts until the 1830's, when women's pockets were finally sewn directly onto garments.

Hickory Dickory Dock*et* - variation of traditional nursery rhyme

Hickory, dickory docket,
The mouse ran into the pocket!
The hand went in, the mouse ran out,
Hickory, dickory docket!

Pease Porridge - variation of a traditional nursery rhyme

Pease porridge hot,
Pease porridge cold,
Pease porridge in the pot,
Nine days old.
Some like it hot,
Some like it cold,
Some like it in the pot,
Nine days old.

Pease porridge hot,
Pease porridge cold,
Pease porridge in the pocket,
Nine days old.
Some like it hot,
Some like it cold,
Some like it in the pocket,
Nine days old.
(Look into your pocket and make a sour face.)
Eeeee Uuuuu YUCK!

Peter Piper - variation of traditional nursery rhyme

If Peter Piper picked a *pocket* of pickled peppers, a *pocket* of pickled peppers Peter Piper picked. But if Peter Piper picked a *pocket* of pickled peppers, where is the *pocket* of pickled peppers Peter Piper picked?

Pat-A-Cake - variation of a traditional nursery rhyme

Pat-a-cake, pat-a-cake, baker's man,
Bake me a cake as fast as you can.
Pat it and prick it, and mark it with a B,
And put it in the oven for Baby and me.

Pat-a-pocket, pat-a-pocket, pocket man,
Sew me a pocket as fast as you can.
Pat it and stuff it, and mark it with a B,
And put it on the pants for Baby and me.

Teddy Bear, Teddy Bear
a variation of a traditional nursery rhyme

Teddy bear, Teddy bear turn around,
Teddy bear, Teddy bear touch the ground,
Teddy bear, Teddy bear hand in your pocket,
Teddy bear, Teddy bear pull out a locket,
Teddy bear, Teddy bear go upstairs,
Teddy bear, Teddy bear say your prayers,
Teddy bear, Teddy bear turn out the light,
Teddy bear, Teddy bear say good night.

Rocket in my Pocket
anonymous

I've got a rocket in my pocket,
I cannot stop to play,
Away it goes!
I've burned my toes!
It's Independence day!

My Pocket - variation of,
"My hat, it has three corners..."

My pocket, it has four corners,
Four corners has my pocket.
If it did not have four corners,
It would not be my pocket!

Sources of other pocket poems and rhymes:

Irving, Jan and Currie, Robin, ***Glad Rags,*** 1987, Libraries Unlimited, Englewood Co. "Pocket Surprise" (p. 224) and "More Hole Than Pocket" (p. 221). Pocket activities (stories, songs, rhymes, games) on pages 219-224, 235, 237.

Irving, Jan and Currie, Robin, ***Raising the Roof,*** 1991, Teachers Ideas Press, Englewood Co. "Pocket Homes" (p. 138) is a poem about different pets that could be found in pockets.

Merriam, Eve, (ill. Hans Wilhelm), ***Blackberry Ink,*** 1985, William Morrow & Co., New York, NY. "Something's in my pocket..." is the first line of a lively poem that mentions many things that aren't in the pocket. Finally the answer is a hole.

Prelutsky, Jack, (ill. Arnold Lobel), ***The Random House Book of Poetry for Children,*** 1983, Random House, New York. Selections about pockets: "Keep a Poem in Your Pocket" by Beatrice Schenk de Regniers, page 226

Simms, Laura, ***There's A Horse In My Pocket,*** Kids' Records, 1987, Toronto, Ontario. A short poem at the end of side two of this cassette tape begins with the title and ends with the statement, "You are the queen and king of your own fairy tale."

Tashjian, Virginia A., (ill. Victoria de Larrea), ***Juba This and Juba That,*** 1969, Little, Brown and Co., Boston, MA. p. 24-29, "What Did You Put in Your Pocket?" by Beatrice Schenk de Regniers. A silly poem that adds something different every day of the week to a pocket, with the refrain repeating all of the items each time: "Slushy Glushy Pudding! Nicy Icy Water! Slurpy Glurpy Ice Cream! etc..." It originally appeared in *Something Special* by Beatrice Schenk de Regniers, 1958, Harcourt, Brace & World, Inc.

Not Rubber Bands

Optional props - Put the following items in your pocket: a piece of notepaper, an eraser, a rock, a little army man, and a tangled wad of brown rubber bands.

Mom was the person who washed clothes at Andy's house. She sorted them according to color and always always always... well, *almost* always remembered to empty all the pockets in all the clothes before tossing them into the washing machine.

(Pull the props one at a time from your pocket.)

She found notes from school that Andy had forgotten to give to her.

She found erasers.

She found rocks.

She found little army men.

And almost always, she found rubber bands, because Andy loved snapping them and was in the habit of picking up every rubber band that he came across.

If the telephone rang while Mom was loading the washing machine, or if Andy suddenly spilled juice on the carpet, or if Mom looked up to see the puppy chewing on furniture, well, if any of those kinds of emergencies happened, then Mom would throw the rest of the things in the machine and miss emptying some pockets. That's when the washing machine clanked and clattered as it swished the clothes around. Andy's clothes would come out decorated with little white pieces of paper, and Mom would always say, "Oh, I wish Andy would learn to check his own pockets!"

One spring, Andy became so interested in collecting creepy crawly things from under the rocks in the backyard, he forgot all about picking up rubber bands. Usually, he carried a collecting jar with him, but sometimes he forgot it in the house. And that's just what happened one day after school.

Andy discovered a huge pile of the longest, slimiest, wiggliest earthworms he had ever seen! But the worms moved so fast, that if he ran into the house to get his collecting jar, they would surely all escape! So Andy grabbed handful after handful of the world's biggest worms and stuck them in his pants pocket. He planned to run right in and get his jar, but Jon from across the street wanted to play catch, and then it was time for supper, and more playing, and reading, and bed... Well, Andy still had not learned to check his pockets at night, so all those fat, juicy earthworms stayed very happily just where they were, in Andy's pants pocket.

When laundry day came, Mom was having a bad day. It seemed like every time she started to do something, she was interrupted, like when the doorbell rang just as she was about to check Andy's pants pocket. So instead of checking his pockets, she threw the pants into the washing machine, slammed down the lid, and dashed away to answer the door.

When she opened the washing machine to remove the wet laundry, she noticed some long brown things clinging to the clothes. "Andy's rubber bands," she said.

But when she reached in for a handful and they began to coil around her fingers, she immediately saw that they were *not* rubber bands.

Mom was never quite able to scrape all the worms off the laundry room ceiling, but she didn't worry about that very much because after all, they were *clean* worms. It is amazing, though, how quickly Andy learned how to check his own pockets every night, and how he never never never... well, *almost* never forgot his collecting jar again.

Options:

1. Make pocketfuls of worms by inserting cooked spaghetti pasta into paper pockets, made by the folding method described on page 41, the lacing method on page 45, or by simply stapling or gluing a patch pocket onto a picture of pants. The pants (see pattern on page 52) may be cut out and decorated, or simply left as a drawing on the paper. Give every child his/her own pocket, or make one large group pocket and let each child put in a "worm". Before introducing this activity (and after telling the story), make a pocketful of worms, but don't tell the children what's in it. Invite one of your more adventurous children to come up and feel what's inside.
2. Get a big box to represent a washing machine. Ask the children to put in their pocketfuls of worms, shake it up, and open it to see if the "worms" stayed in the pockets.
3. Tell the story again with the children acting out the parts of Mom, Andy, and a puppy. Other children can pretend to be rocks in the backyard, and still others can pretend to be the washing machine by sitting and facing each other, holding hands. Ask some children to make the sound effects: ringing telephone, doorbell, washing machine sounds, and Mom screaming about the worms.
4. Ask, "Who remembers to empty your own pockets? What kinds of things has your mom or dad found in your pockets? Do you think this story might have really happened? Why do you think Andy suddenly learned to check his own pockets? Can you think of some other things besides worms that should not go into pockets?"
5. Sing the song, "We All Put Our Clothes On" (it has a verse about checking pockets) on page 57, and read the poems, "A Pocket" (page 15), "Pockets" (page 17), "Stuff Your Pocket" (page 18), "Ten Things" (page 29), "Pease Porridge" (page 34), and "What Did You Put In Your Pocket?" by Beatrice Schenk de Regniers (source found on page 36).

?

What is the best way to make a pocket last?
Make the coat and the pants and the shirt and everything else...first!

Is it better to draw a picture with an empty pocket or a full pocket?
Neither, draw with a pencil instead!

Penny's Paper Pocket

Required prop: A penny and a square piece of paper.

Not far from here, a girl named Penny lives with her mom and dad in a house right next door to her Grandma Pen. When Penny was old enough to go to school, some of the other girls and boys, who had names like Chris and Derrick and Stephanie, laughed when they heard her name.

"Do you live in a piggy bank?" they wanted to know.

"Can we buy a gum ball with you?" they wondered.

Penny had never thought about her name before. After school she decided to ask her mom why she was named Penny.

"We named you after your Grandma Pen, honey. Your Grandma's name is Penny, and she is one of the brightest people we know."

"Did she ever live in a piggy bank?" asked Penny.

"No," said her mom, "but she worked in one once."

Next Penny asked her dad why she had been named Penny.

"It's good luck to find a penny," he said. "And we've had nothing but good luck since you were born."

Penny decided to go to Grandma Pen's house to show her the picture she had painted that day in school. On the way, she noticed a shiny round coin on the sidewalk.

"A penny!" she said. "But where can I put it? I don't have a pocket." She brought it to Grandma Pen, who always knew what to do about everything.

"You are a lucky girl today," said Grandma Pen. "Let's just put your penny in that pretty picture of yours so that you won't lose it on the way home." Grandma pen put the penny in the middle of the picture and folded the bottom edge up like this *(demonstrate with fold #1)*.

Fold #1 - The penny folded inside the picture.

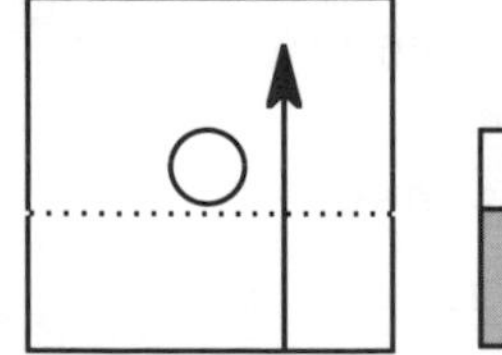

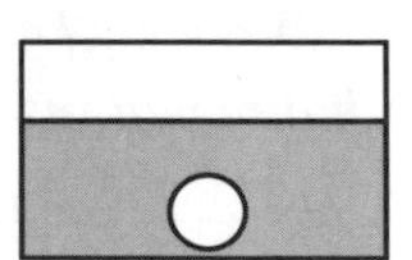

After a snack of cider and doughnut holes, Penny started to go home. But when she stepped out of Grandma Pen's house, the penny rolled out of the side, like this. *(Let the penny roll out onto the floor.)* So Penny decided to fold that edge back, like this *(demonstrate with fold #2)*, and put the penny back inside.

Fold #2 - The picture with one side folded back.

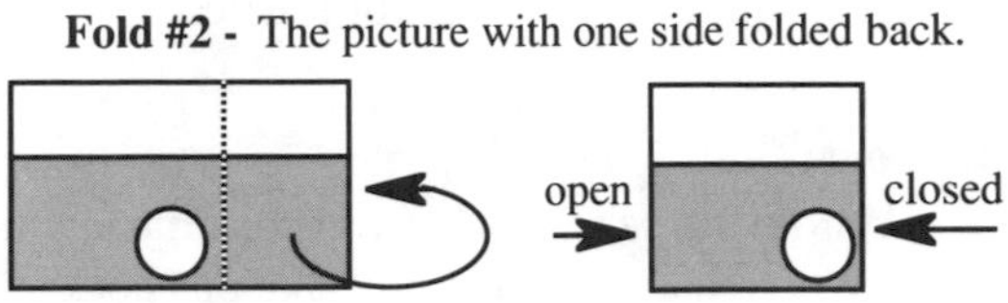

As you can imagine, Penny didn't get very far before the penny rolled out of the other side. She decided to fold that side, too. *(Demonstrate with fold #3)*. It took a while to find the bright coin again, but Penny finally spotted it in the grass next to the sidewalk. She slipped it through the top, like this *(demonstrate by replacing the penny through the opening)*.

Fold #3 - The picture with two sides folded back.

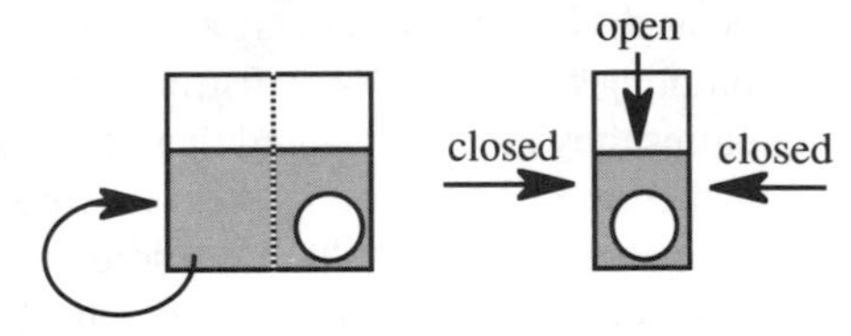

As Penny pulled on the door to her house, she dropped the paper and the penny slipped out of the top opening. "This penny keeps trying to get away, but I'm going to keep finding it," she said. She picked it up, slipped it through the opening, and folded the top edge down so that it would never roll out again. *(Demonstrate with fold #4)*.

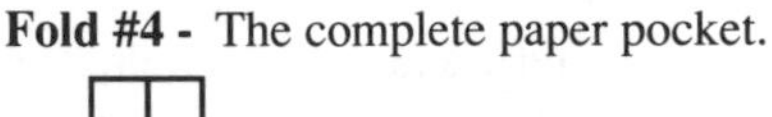

Fold #4 - The complete paper pocket.

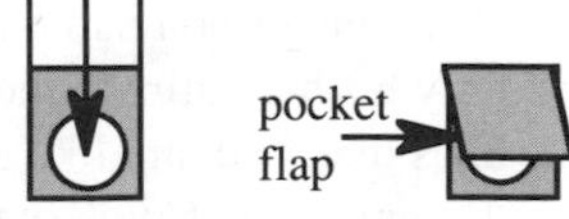

When she got inside, she showed her parents her paper pocket with the penny in it.

"Look Dad! Look Mom! I'm *really* lucky! I found this penny four times! And I guess I am like Grandma Pen, too. Because I figured out how to make this pocket all by myself."

From then on, whenever any of the children at school made fun of her name, Penny just smiled proudly and said, "My name makes sense. I'm bright and lucky as a penny, so if you want good luck, try to find me! You're *it*!"

Then she would run away and hide, and start a game of hide and seek that was so much fun, everyone felt like they really did have the best luck ever.

Options:

1. Unfold the paper pocket you constructed during the story and ask, "Who remembers how to make this pocket? What was the first thing that Grandma Pen did?" Review each step, reconstructing the pocket as the children remember the sequence of folding steps. Build it one more time as they act as "teachers" and tell you what to do without any prompting from you. Next distribute paper (or let them use one of the pictures they drew or painted that day) and construct the paper pocket together as a group, step by step. Always refer back to the story events. This association will help the children remember what comes next. Do not be concerned that the children's pockets end up as different sizes. Instead, value their differences, complimenting their independent efforts. Challenge them to teach their older siblings or parents how to fold the paper pockets at home. Encourage them to bring back home-folded ones for show-and-tell.
2. Hide pennies throughout the room before you tell the story. Go on a penny hunt. Ask the children to bring the pennies to a centralized basket or bowl. Give each child a penny to take home in their paper pockets.
3. Recite "Lucy Locket" (page 34) and "A Pocket" (page 15).
4. Ask, "How did Penny feel when the children made fun of her name? How did Penny feel when she found out how special her name was? Should we laugh at people's names?"
5. Ask, "Are any of you named after someone in your family?" Let each child say his/her entire name. This is a good lead in to name activities or games like, "Square like a Pocket" on page 67.
6. Try "Disappearing Coin" (page 80) and sing "In A Pocket Clemintine" (page 58) and "The Pockets on the Bus Song" (page 59).

What always has an eye open but
can't see anything?
A needle!

The Pocket Holes of Pocketville

Once upon a time, there was a little town by the name of Pocketville where all the people wore pockets on their pants, shirts, coats, sweaters, socks, and yes, even on their underwear.

They carried big heavy things in big heavy pockets.

They carried medium things in medium pockets.

They carried little flat things in little flat pockets.

And they saved their tiny little secret pockets for tiny little secret things, like dreams and funny songs and of course, their needle and thread. Everyone in Pocketville, even the youngest child, knew how to sew because naturally, whenever you have a lot of pockets, you also have a lot of pocket holes to fix.

Pocketville people had plenty of thread and never worried about wasting it. They gave away colors they didn't like, threw out tangles they couldn't loosen, and tossed long strands of thread into the air just to see which way the wind was blowing. They never thought that they would ever run out of thread.

But then one day, the thread makers, who lived in the next town, decided that they were tired of making thread. They stopped making thread, packed their suitcases, loaded them into their cars, and drove away to the beach. They stayed at the beach for a long, long time and made no plans to ever go back to making thread.

At first, Pocketville people had plenty of thread stored up in their sewing boxes, but then one by one, they began to run out. More and more pockets had more and more pocket holes.

The few people who still had thread wouldn't share their thread with anyone. They stopped giving away unpopular colors. They stopped throwing away tangles and knots. And everyone began to protect their pockets by not filling them up quite so much and by not putting in sharp things that would make pocket holes. But how would they carry all the things that no longer fit in pockets?

They tried stacking things in their arms, but the things tipped and crashed.

They tried balancing things on their heads, but the things slid and smashed.

They tried pulling things in wagons, pushing things in carts, and rolling things along the ground, but nothing seemed to work as well as pockets.

Finally, the Pocketville people decided that they should learn to make their own thread. They asked one of the thread makers to come back from the beach to help them get started. Although it took a lot of practice and hard work, they eventually learned how to make thread that was just right for fixing pocket holes. And the thread makers were happy too because they liked the beach so much, that they decided to move there permanently in order to make rope for fishing nets.

Now that the Pocketville people had plenty of thread, they went back to the happy days of carrying everything in their pockets, without worrying about making too many pocket holes. But they were careful never to waste thread again, and to this day, if you want to know which way the wind is blowing in Pocketville, don't throw a strand of thread in the air to find out. Look at the leaves on the trees instead.

Options:

1. Ask, "Has anyone ever had a hole in their pocket? Does someone have a pocket hole now? What kinds of things can be lost out of pocket holes? What kinds of things would stay in a pocket, even if it had a hole in it?"
2. Sing the songs, "There's a Hole in the Bottom of My Pocket" (page 61) and, "There's a Hole In The Pocket" (page 54). Read the poems, "Cobbler, Cobbler" (page 23), "Pat-A-Cake" (page 35), and "Something's In My Pocket" by Eve Merriam (source on page 36).
3. Sew two squares of fabric together with a needle and thread. Have two 6" squares and one threaded needle for each child. Help them get started by knotting the thread and pulling it through the first time. Use a straight stitch, in one side, out the other. Younger children can make

pockets by lacing two paper squares together. Punch an even number of holes through two paper squares. Sew with yarn that has one end knotted and the other end wrapped in masking tape.

4. Use this story as part of a unit about ecology and conservation. Talk about not wasting the things that we use everyday, such as water or electricity. Ask, "Have you ever run out of something at home? How did it feel to not have enough? What did you do? What else could the people of Pocketville have done to solve their pocket hole problem?"

The Pocket Farm

One day in October, a curious boy named Brian sat on his bedroom floor staring at his next door neighbor's backyard. Since there was nothing interesting happening at his house, Brian was wondering what was going on over at the Taylors'. They didn't have any children and hardly ever came outside. His mom said that they were pocket people, kind of like artists. They worked at home in their basement, making fancy pockets for fancy suits and fancy wedding dresses.

Brian hated weddings, but he loved the Taylors' trees. They had sprawling oak trees that bombed him with the world's biggest acorns. They had a maple tree with the best climbing branches all the way to its top. And they had drooping pine trees that Brian could tunnel under and disappear so well that even his dog couldn't find him.

Like most days in October, it was windy. Colorful leaves were parachuting down from the treetops and cartwheeling from yard to yard. But the leaves over in the Taylors' yard seemed bigger than usual, and Brian thought that they were oddly shaped. They were squarish and doubled over, like pockets.

Maybe they were pockets.

Maybe the Taylors got their pockets from their trees.

Maybe the trees he loved to play in were really just part of one big pocket farm...

And that's when Mr. and Mrs. Taylor came dashing out into their back yard with floppy collecting bags slung over their shoulders. They were shouting and laughing, darting around, scooping up as many of these oddly shaped leaves as quickly as they could. Brian opened his window so that he could hear what they said.

"Get that one!" shouted Mrs. Taylor. "It's the color brown that we need."

"A dream come true! Just what we've been hoping for!" shrieked Mr. Taylor. They linked arms, twirling and spinning with joy.

Brian had never in his whole life seen grown-ups acting like this! He was not going to sit still and watch while all this celebrating was going on outside. He grabbed some socks, leaped downstairs to find his play shoes at the bottom of the toybox, hurried into the garage to get his jacket, ran back in to go to the bathroom, searched through the closet for a paper bag, and bolted into the backyard to help the Taylors pick up pocket leaves.

But by that time, they were gone. There were no falling pockets. There were no dancing Taylors. The October leaves somersaulted. Squirrels chuckled. Roving bands of black birds flitted away. All was quiet as usual.

Even after all that running around getting ready, Brian wasn't too disappointed. At least now he had a bag for collecting a few of the world's biggest acorns. And maybe the Taylors weren't picking up pockets after all, he thought. Maybe they came out just to play with him, and they got tired of waiting and went back inside.

Next time, Brian was going to put on his shoes and jacket before he watched the Taylor's house. They didn't come outside very often, but when they did, they sure were funny and he wanted to be ready for anything!

Options:

1. Ask, "Have you ever seen leaves falling from the trees? What are some ways that leaves can be used? Do you think that Brian really saw pocket leaves, or did he just imagine them? Close your eyes and pretend to be a leaf. Imagine what it feels like to be a leaf falling from a tree or cartwheeling from place to place. Are you light or heavy? Does it hurt when you hit the ground? What do you see? What do you hear? Is it hot or cold outside?"
2. Make pocket leaves. Use the pattern on page 51, or make your own with leaf rubbings. Pre-cut or ask the children to cut out two large leaves. Decorate realistically with leaf veins or creatively, however the children want their pocket leaves to look. Hold the two leaves together and punch an even number of holes in the sides, leaving the top of the leaf open. Wrap masking tape around one end of an 24" strand of yarn, line up the holes, and pull the yarn through the first holes, weaving the yarn in and out until the last holes are sewn. Leave about 8" loose at the first hole to be tied off later with the ending yarn for a handle.
3. Read the poems on pages 26 - 27, "Making Friends" (page 20), "Peter Piper" (page 34), and "Cobbler, Cobbler" (page 23). Sing "Pawpaw Patch" on page 53.

Picture storybooks about pockets

*Indicates especially wonderful!

Barrett, Judi, (ill. Julia Noonan),** ***Peter's Pocket, 1974, Atheneum, New York, NY. Peter is almost four years old and loves to collect things throughout the day. He doesn't have enough clothes with pockets, so his mother constructs removable pockets that eventually become mushy, stuffy, heavy, holey, and wet. A pattern is included for making simple pin-on pockets.

Carter, David A.,** ***What's In My Pocket?, 1989, G. P. Putnam's Sons, New York, NY. A pop-up & peek-in book featuring five colorful animals with things to eat in their pockets.

Caudill, Rebecca, (ill. Evaline Ness), ***A Pocketful of Cricket***, 1964, Henry Holt and Co., New York, NY. Jay walks through the countryside collecting souvenirs for his pocket, including a cricket. The cricket begins to sing at school, disturbing the class, but when the teacher notices that Jay really likes the cricket, she uses it as a show and tell lesson. The text is rather long for a preschool group, but it makes a good one-to-one read.

Cazet, Denys, ***A Fish In His Pocket,*** 1987, Orchard Books, a Division of Franklin Watts, Inc., New York, NY. Russell drops his math book in the pond on the way to school and when his teacher discovers a fish in it, he puts the fish into his pocket until after school, when he places it in a paperfolded boat and returns it to the water.

Christian, Mary Blount, (ill. Jane Dyer), ***Penrod's Pants***, 1986, Macmillan Publishing Co., New York, NY. The first of five short stories is about a new pair of pants with four pockets, one containing a five-dollar bill. Penrod Porcupine and his friend Griswold Bear go shopping for another pair, but can't find any with money in the pockets.

Dorling Kindersley Book, ***My First Look at Clothes***, 1991, (My First Look At series) Random House, Inc., New York, NY. Large color photos of an assortment of children's clothing, many containing, but not necessarily featuring, pockets.

Foster, Doris Van Liew, (ill. Talivaldis Stubis), ***A Pocketful of Seasons***, 1961, Lothrop, Lee & Shepard, New York, NY. Each season, Andy picks up something for his pocket as the farmer works in his fields. At the end of the year, Andy has something from each of the seasons in his pocket.

Freeman, Don,** ***A Pocket For Corduroy, 1978, The Viking Press, New York, NY. Corduroy the stuffed bear searches for a pocket of his own at the laundromat, gets lost and left behind, and has soapy adventures throughout the night. *(More Story Stretchers* by Shirley C. Raines and Robert J. Canady, 1991, Gryphon House, Mt. Rainier, Maryland has activities about this story on page 146-147.)

Goins, Ellen H.,** ***David's Pockets, 1972, Steck-Vaughn Co., Austin, TX. A boy fills his pockets with treasures from nature, observing many animals and insects along the way.

Harshman, Marc & Collins, Bonnie, (ill. Toni Goffe), ***Rocks In My Pockets***, 1991, Cobblehill Books, New York, NY. The Woods family live on a rocky farm at the top of a mountain where they always carry rocks in their pockets so the wind won't blow them away. These well rubbed rocks become treasures when city people begin to buy them.

Lobel, Arnold, ***Frog and Toad Are Friends***, 1970, Harper Collins, New York, NY. "A Lost Button," the third of five short stories, describes how Frog tries to help Toad find his button. Toad stores all the wrong buttons in his pocket until he finally finds his at home.

Marshall, Janet Perry,** ***Ohmygosh My Pocket, 1992, Boyds Mills Press, Honesdale, PA. Colorful pictures with bold lines are attractive for very young children. A child finally decides what to carry in his pocket: a frog.

McClintock, Mike, (ill. Leonard Kessler), ***What Have I Got?***, 1961, Harper & Row, New York, NY. A boy shows all the things he has in his pocket and then demonstrates what he can do with them (rhyming verse).

Merriam, Eve, (ill. Harriet Sherman),** ***What Can You Do With A Pocket?, 1964, Alfred A. Knopf, Inc., New York, NY. Many ideas for what can be in pockets are given, and how they can be used in imaginative ways. Lively sounds and illustrations make the suggestions jump from the pages. "A pocket is your treasure place. You can keep whatever you want there, because it's your own inside house and everything in it belongs just to you."

Neitzel, Shirley, (ill. Nancy Winslow Parker), ***The Jacket I Wear In The Snow***, 1989, Greenwillow Books, New York, NY. A brightly illustrated poem and rebus, easily solved, about getting all dressed for the snow, only to encounter frustration. Mother comes to the rescue. The jeans have pockets, but they are not a part of the plot.

Pragoff, Fiona, ***Clothes***, 1989, Doubleday, New York, NY. A wirebound book of colorful photographs of children's clothes. The overalls have five brightly colored pockets.

Ravilious, Robin, ***Two in a Pocket***, 1991, Little, Brown and Company, Boston, MA. A dormouse and a wren share a home in an old coat pocket and must be wary of a stalking cat. Finally, the farmer takes the old coat to the field to make a scarecrow and the animals aren't afraid anymore.

Rice, Eve, (ill. Nancy Winslow Parker),** ***Peter's Pockets, 1989, Greenwillow Books, New York, NY. Peter finds wonderful treasures, but his new pants have no pockets until his mother adds a pocket for each of his discoveries.

Willard, Barbara, (ill. Mary Russon), ***The Pocket Mouse***, 1969, Alfred A. Knopf, Inc., New York, NY. Colin keeps a stuffed mouse in his pocket during a visit to his grandfather. He leaves his jacket in a field, and a real mouse enters. He takes care of it for a while, but then returns it to the wild. The text is too long for a story hour, but paraphrased or used one-to-one, it is a good story.

Wright, Betty Ren, (ill. Jared D. Lee), ***Roger's Upside-Down Day***, 1979, Western Publishing Company, Inc., Racine, WI. Roger's pockets empty out when he has a strange feeling and begins to walk on the ceiling. Finally, the wind changes and he returns to normal (rhyming verse).

Sources for more pocket stories to tell:

Catron, Elaine and Parks, Barbara, (Ill. Jane Shasky), ***Super Story Telling***, 1986, T. S. Denison & Co., Minneapolis, MN. pages 141-153 have four short rhymes called "pocket stories" that require pouches made from patterns of a fat old lady, Santa, a witch, and the Easter bunny. Most are counting rhymes.

Irving, Jan and Currie, Robin, (Ill. Tom Henrichsen), ***Glad Rags: Stories and Activities Featuring Clothes For Children***, 1987, Libraries Unlimited, Inc., Littleton, Co. pages 216-221 have stories, rhymes, and songs about pockets.

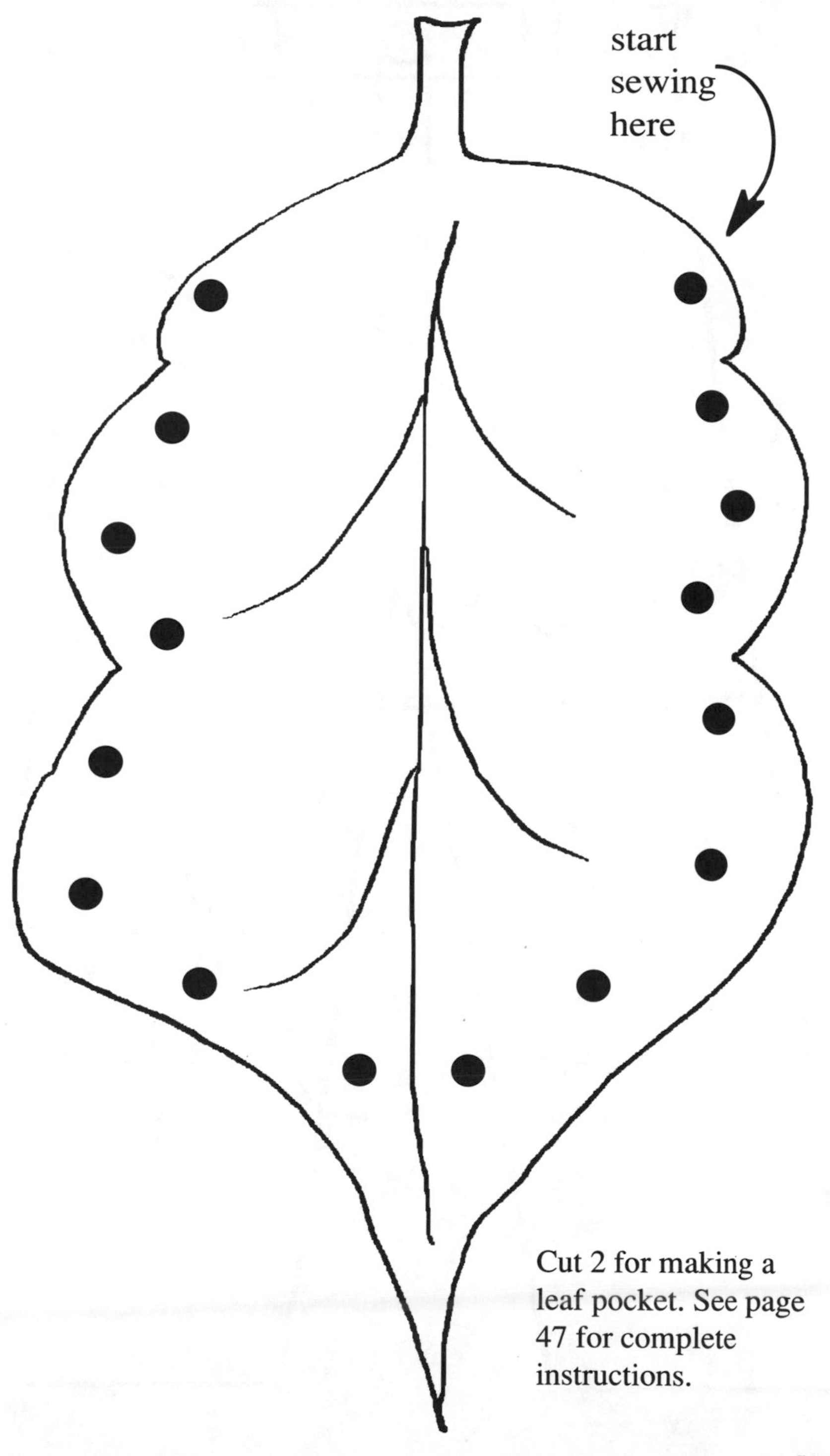

Cut 2 for making a leaf pocket. See page 47 for complete instructions.

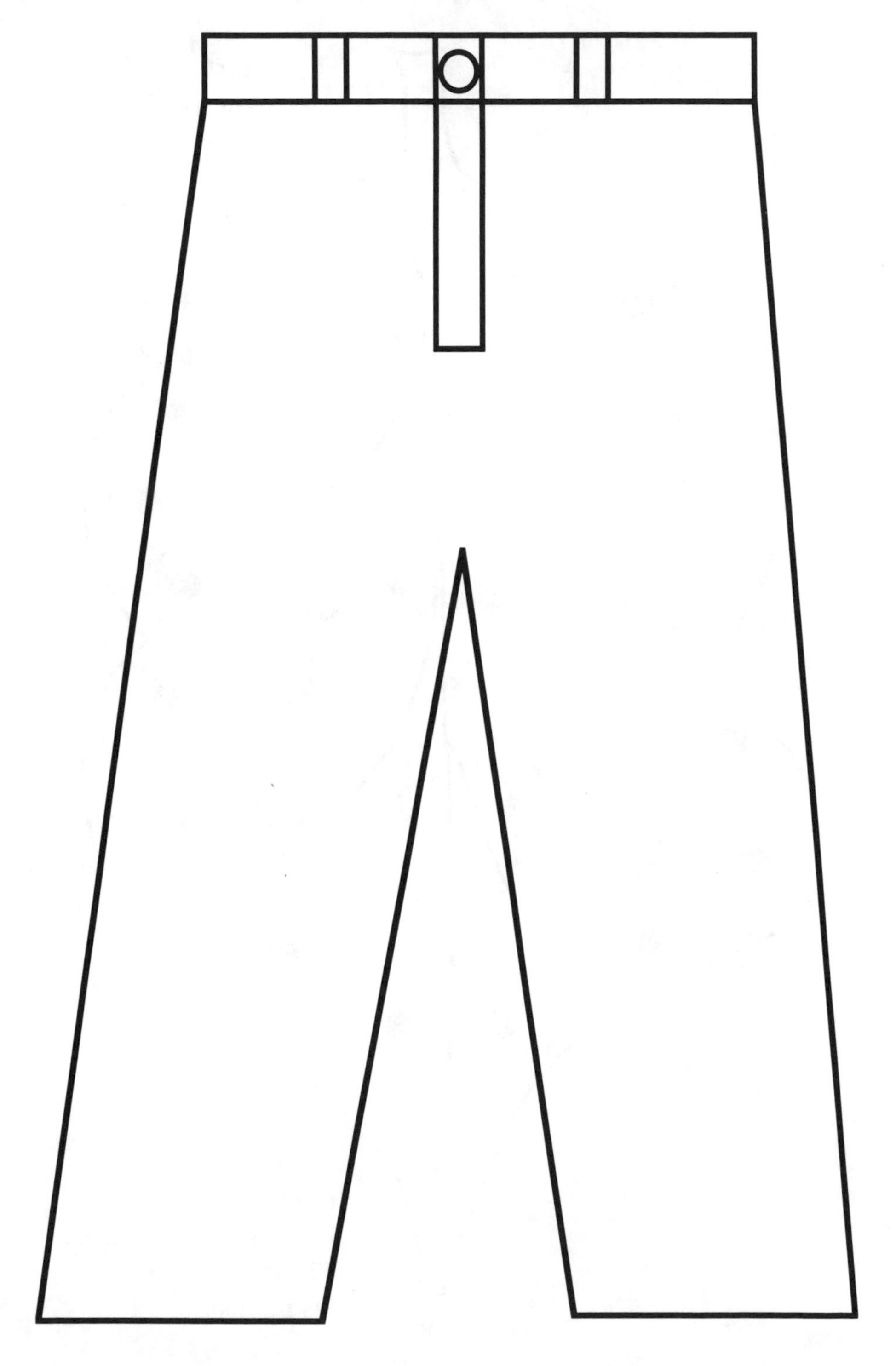

Silly Songs For Pocket Fun

Pawpaw Patch - traditional folksong of the Southern U.S.

Where oh where is pretty little Sally?
Where oh where is pretty little Sally?
Where oh where is pretty little Sally?
Way down yonder in the pawpaw patch.

Come on, boys, let's go find her.
Come on, boys, let's go find her.
Come on, boys, let's go find her.
Way down yonder in the pawpaw patch.

Picking up pawpaws, put 'em in your pocket.
Picking up pawpaws, put 'em in your pocket.
Picking up pawpaws, put 'em in your pocket.
Way down yonder in the pawpaw patch.

Options:

1. A pawpaw is an oblong, yellow fruit which grows on tropical trees in the central and southern United States, Hawaii, and the Philippines. If your students are not familiar with it, you might substitute *pumpkin* for *paw-paw* in the fall; in summer, substitute a vegetable suggested by the children; in winter, snowballs; in spring, tulips.
2. Change *boys* to *children, girls* or *kids* (whichever fits your group) and personalize the song by using one of your children's names instead of "Sally".
3. This song can be used as a simple circle dance, with one child in the middle for the first verse, pretending to pick up something to put in her pocket (use that child's name instead of "Sally") and the others holding hands and circling round. On the second verse, the circle walks in and out of the middle, raising up their arms as they go in, lowering them as they go out. On the third verse, all release hands to pick up imaginary paw-paws and put them in their pockets. The child in the middle or the teacher can select a new "Sally" for another time.
4. To emphasize fine motor skills, scatter cotton balls, wadded up paper scraps, dried peas, or packing peanuts to represent paw-paws, so that the children actually pick them up.

Busy Fingers

(sing to the tune of "Here We Go Round the Mulberry Bush")

1. This is the way my fingers stand,
   (Hold palms face out, with fingers straight and still.)
   fingers stand, fingers stand,
   This is the way my fingers stand,
   so early in the morning*.

2. This is the way my fingers dance...
   (Flit them around.)

3. This is the way my fingers hide...
   (Slip them into real or pretend pockets.)

4. This is the way my fingers rest...
   (Fold them on your lap.)

*substitute another time of day or the name of your building.

There's A Hole In The Pocket

adaptation of traditional U. S. folksong

(sing with boys and girls alternating verses to the tune of "There's A Hole In The Bucket")

Boys sing, then....	**Girls sing....**
There's a hole in the pocket Dear Liza, dear Liza, There's a hole in the pocket Dear Liza, a hole.	Mend the hole then, dear Georgie, Dear Georgie, dear Georgie, Mend the hole then, dear Georgie, Dear Georgie, the hole.
With what shall I mend it? Dear Liza, dear Liza, With what shall I mend it? Dear Liza, the hole.	With a string then, dear Georgie, Dear Georgie, dear Georgie, With a string then, dear Georgie, Dear Georgie, a string.

Boys:
If the string be too long?
Dear Liza, dear Liza,
If the string be too long?
Dear Liza, the string.

Girls:
Cut the string then, dear Georgie,
Dear Georgie, dear Georgie,
Cut the string then, dear Georgie,
Dear Georgie, the string.

With what shall I cut it?
Dear Liza, dear Liza,
With what shall I cut it?
Dear Liza, the string.

With a knife then, dear Georgie,
Dear Georgie, dear Georgie,
With a knife then, dear Georgie,
Dear Georgie, a knife.

If the knife be too dull?
Dear Liza, dear Liza,
If the knife be too dull?
Dear Liza, the knife.

Whet the knife then, dear Georgie,
Dear Georgie, dear Georgie,
Whet the knife then, dear Georgie,
Dear Georgie, the knife.

With what shall I whet it?
Dear Liza, dear Liza,
With what shall I whet it?
Dear Liza, the knife.

With a stone then, dear Georgie,
Dear Georgie, dear Georgie,
With a stone then, dear Georgie,
Dear Georgie, the stone.

In what shall I fetch it?
Dear Liza, dear Liza,
In what shall I fetch it?
Dear Liza, the stone.

With the pocket, dear Georgie,
Dear Georgie, dear Georgie,
With the pocket, dear Georgie,
Dear Georgie, the pocket.

Spoken by all: *But there's a hole in the pocket!*

Where Oh Where Has My Pocket Gone?

(sing to the tune of "Where Has My Little Dog Gone?")

Oh where, oh where has my pocket gone?
Oh where, oh where could it be?
With it's sides cut short and its string cut long,
Oh where, oh where can it be?

Where Is Thumpkin? - traditional U.S. folksong

1. Where is Thumpkin? Where is Thumpkin?
   Here I am. Here I am.
   How are you this morning?
   Very well, I thank you.
   Hide away. Hide away. (*Hide thumbs in pocket.)*

2. Where is Pointer? Where is Pointer?...
3. Where is Tall Man? Where is Tall Man?...
4. Where is Ring Man? Where is Ring Man?...
5. Where is Baby? Where is Baby?...

6. Where are all the men? Where are all the men?
   Here we are. Here we are.
   How are you this morning?
   Very well, I thank you.
   Hide away. Hide away. *(Hide all fingers in pocket.)*

Where's Your Pocket?

(sing to the tune of "Are You Sleeping?")

Where's your pocket?
Where's your pocket?
Find it now. Find it now.
What would you put in it?
What would you put in it?
Tell us now. Tell us now.

Sing the song together as a group and then call on each child to stand and show his pocket and name something that he would like to put in it. If a child isn't wearing a pocket that day, let him tell about another article of clothing that does have a pocket in it. Repeat the song often, varying the volume and tempo to give variety.

We All Put Our Clothes On - CPK

(Pantomime the motions as you sing.)

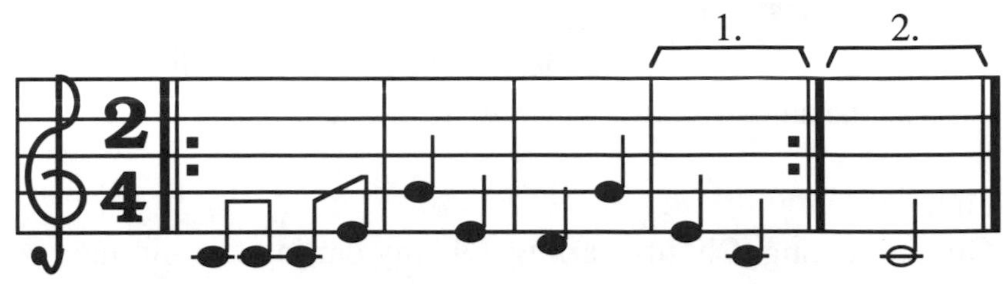

1. We all put our pants on, pants on, pants on,
   We all put our pants on, just like......................this.

2. We all put our shirts on, shirts on, shirts on,
   We all put our shirts on, just like.................... this.

3. We all put our socks on, socks on, socks on,
   We all put our socks on, just like .... this.

4. We all put our shoes on, shoes on, shoes on,
   We all put our shoes on, just like ....this.

5. We all check our pockets, pockets, pockets,
   We all check our pockets, just like..................this.

Ten Little Pockets - CPK

(sing to the tune of "Ten Little Indians")

This counting song works well with a ten-pocket apron or pocket board (p. 115) or with other counting rhymes (p. 29-32).

One little, two little, three little pockets,
four little, five little, six little pockets,
seven little, eight little, nine little pockets,
ten little pockets here.

Ten little, nine little, eight little pockets...

In A Pocket Clemintine - CPK

(sing to the traditional U. S. folksong "Clemintine")

1. In a pocket, in some blue jeans, excavating for a dime,
   Was the hand of a little girl, by the name of Clemintine.

chorus:

Oh, my darling, Oh, my darling, Oh, my darling Clemintine.
(Hold both hands over your heart for the first line.)
You are lost and gone forever, dreadful sorry, Clemintine!
(Hold one hand on your forehead in a mournful gesture.)

2. Found a nickel, found a penny, but no dime was there to see.
   Look again and stop that crying, or you'll never be happy.

3. Looked again and found a tiny little coin, it was a dime,
   At the phone, it was so sad, started crying one more time.

4. It took a quarter to make a phone call, not the tiny little dime. Had to dig in the blue jean pocket, hopefully for the last time.

5. Found a quarter, made a phone call, got her Mommy on the line. And that's how a blue jean pocket saved a girl named Clemintine!

last chorus:

Oh, my darling, Oh, my darling, Oh, my darling Clemintine.
(Hold hands over heart, as usual.)
You are found and found forever, very happy, Clemintine!
(Open arms in a wide embrace.)

Options:

1. Take the appropriate coins out of your pocket during the song and pantomime the motions. Encourage the children to sing the chorus and do the motions with you.

2. Set the coins out. Ask, "Where is the penny? What color is it? Are there other brown (copper) coins? Which is the biggest? Which is the smallest? Which is used for phone calls?" This song is a good lead-in to money identification units.
3. Ask, "How does Clemintine feel when she is lost? How does she feel when she is found? What should we do if we are lost? Who knows their phone number? Who knows how to use a pay phone?" This song also makes a nice lead-in to a safety unit, emphasizing learning home phone numbers and role-playing what to do if a child is lost.
4. Trace and cut out paper coins and make any one of the paper pockets on pages 25, 38, 42, or 52. Repeat the song, with the children reaching into their pockets for their coins. Use the coins in other activities.

The Pockets on the Bus

(sing to the tune of "The People On The Bus"

The pockets on the bus go ching, ching, ching,
Ching, ching, ching, ching, ching, ching.
The pockets on the bus go ching, ching, ching,
All through the town.

2. The pockets on the train go chug, chug, chug...
3. The pockets on the plane go up and down...
4. The pockets on the fire truck go rush, rush, rush...
5. The pockets on the bike go push, push, push...
6. The pockets on the hike say, "Fill me up..."

I'm A Little Pocket - CPK

(sing to the tune of "I'm A Little Teapot")

Sing the song with a real pocket, or simply pantomime the motions. Dump out props for your next activity, or develop a group story with the items that fall out *(see #4 on page 67)*.

I'm a little pocket, short and wide,
Here is my opening, here is my side.
When I get all filled up, then I shout,
Tip me over and dump me out!

Go In And Out The Pocket - CPK

(sing to the tune of "Go In And Out The Window")

Slip a hand in and out of a real or imaginary pocket. Pantomime putting in the objects, using tiny fingers for the locket, big round arms for the rocket, and medium movement for the socket. Some children won't know what a locket or socket are, so be prepared to show them with real examples.

Go in and out the pocket.
Go in and out the pocket.
Go in and out the pocket
As we have done before.

We will put in the locket.
We will put in the locket.
We will put in the locket
As we have done before.

We will put in the rocket.
We will put in the rocket.
We will put in the rocket
As we have done before.

We will put in the socket.
We will put in the socket.
We will put in the socket
As we have done before.

Now put away the pocket.
Now put away the pocket.
Now put away the pocket
As we have done before.

Options:

1. Ask, "What really fits in pockets? What would never fit? Let's sing the song again, but this time, I'll ask for your ideas about what to put in." Repeat so that each child gets a chance to make a suggestion.
2. Ask, "What is special about the words *pocket, locket, rocket, and socket*? Can we think of three other things that rhyme that might or might not fit into a pocket?" Decide which would fit and which wouldn't fit. Then sing your new version:

   We will put in the key.
   We will put in the bee.
   We will put in the knee.
   As we have done before.

   Other possibilities with short vowels are rock, sock, lock; pan, can, van; hill, pill, bill; jet, net, pet; bun, sun, gun. Emphasize the vowel sounds you are currently working on.

There's A Hole In The Bottom Of My Pocket

(sing to the tune of "There's A Hole in The Bottom of the Sea")

There's a hole in the bottom of my pocket, there's a hole in the bottom of my pocket, there's a hole, there's a hole, there's a hole in the bottom of my pocket.

There's a rock in the hole in the bottom of my pocket, there's a rock in the hole in the bottom of my pocket, there's a rock, there's a rock, there's a rock in the hole in the bottom of my pocket.

(Continue all the verses in the same way.)

3. There's a feather on the rock in the hole at the bottom of my pocket....
4. There's some gum on the feather on the rock in the hole of my pocket...
5. There's a hand stuck on the gum on the feather on the rock in the hole of my pocket...
6. There's an arm on the hand stuck on the gum on the feather on the rock in the hole of my pocket...
7. There's a shoulder on the arm on the hand stuck on the gum on the feather on the rock in the hole of my pocket...
8. There's a neck on the shoulder on the arm on the hand stuck on the gum on the feather on the rock in the hole of my pocket...
9. Oh oh!...It's Mom's head on the neck on the shoulder on the arm on the hand stuck on the gum on the feather on the rock in the hole of my pocket...

Old MacDonald Had A Pocket - CPK

(sing to the tune of "Old MacDonald Had A Farm")

Old MacDonald had a pocket, E-I-E-I-O,
And in that pocket he had a wrench, E-I-E-I-O.
With a crank-crank here and a crank-crank there,
Here a crank, there a crank, everywhere a crank-crank.
Old MacDonald had a pocket, E-I-E-I-O.

Old MacDonald had a pocket, E-I-E-I-O,
And in that pocket he had a hammer, E-I-E-I-O.
With a pound-pound here and a pound-pound there,
Here a pound, there a pound, everywhere a pound-pound.
A crank-crank here and a crank-crank there,
Here a crank, there a crank, everywhere a crank-crank.
Old MacDonald had a pocket, E-I-E-I-O.

Old MacDonald had a pocket, E-I-E-I-O,
And in that pocket he had a key, E-I-E-I-O.
With a lock-lock here and a lock-lock there,
Here a lock, there a lock, everywhere a lock-lock.
A pound-pound here and a pound-pound there,
Here a pound, there a pound, everywhere a pound-pound.
A crank-crank here and a crank-crank there,
Here a crank, there a crank, everywhere a crank-crank.
Old MacDonald had a pocket, E-I-E-I-O.

Old MacDonald had a pocket, E-I-E-I-O,
And in that pocket he had a paintbrush, E-I-E-I-O.
With a paint-paint here and a paint-paint there,
Here a paint, there a paint, everywhere a paint-paint.
A lock-lock here and a lock-lock there,
Here a lock, there a lock, everywhere a lock-lock.
A pound-pound here and a pound-pound there,
Here a pound, there a pound, everywhere a pound-pound.

A crank-crank here and a crank-crank there,
Here a crank, there a crank, everywhere a crank-crank.
Old MacDonald had a pocket, E-I-E-I-O.

Old MacDonald had a pocket, E-I-E-I-O,
And in that pocket he had a screwdriver, E-I-E-I-O.
With a turn-turn here and a turn-turn there,
Here a turn, there a turn, everywhere a turn-turn.
A paint-paint here and a paint-paint there,
Here a paint, there a paint, everywhere a paint-paint.
A lock-lock here and a lock-lock there,
Here a lock, there a lock, everywhere a lock-lock.
A pound-pound here and a pound-pound there,
Here a pound, there a pound, everywhere a pound-pound.
A crank-crank here and a crank-crank there,
Here a crank, there a crank, everywhere a crank-crank.
Old MacDonald had a pocket, E-I-E-I-O.

Options:

1. Pantomime each action while you sing, increasing the tempo at the end.
2. Bring actual samples of each tool. Select one child to be in charge of each tool, so that when that tool comes up in the song, that child should stand and hold up his tool. Leave plenty of space between each child, so that no one gets hurt with the heavier tools.
3. This is a good lead-in to picture story books about farms, over-alls, tools or tool aprons, such as *Katy No-Pocket* by Emmy Payne, source on page 99.
4. Ask, "What else would Old MacDonald have in his pockets? Are there farm animals small enough to fit in pockets? What sounds do they make?" Some possibilities are puppies, kittens, piglets, chicks, or mice. Read *Two In A Pocket* by Robin Ravilious, source on page 49. This is a story of how two animals found a home in a farmer's coat pocket.

***Cassette recording about pockets**

Wise, Joe, *Pockets: Songs For Little People*, G. I. A. Publications, Inc., Chicago, IL. The lead song on side one has an upbeat, humorous song about the singer's pockets. The chorus, "I've got five pockets in my over-alls..." repeats frequently, and has banjo & percussion accompaniment.

Learning and Laughing With Pocket Games

What's Inside The Pocket?

Find pictures, toys, or actual objects to put into a pocket for the game. Use a pocket board or apron with many pockets (see p. 115) or an apron with just one pocket where you turn your back to the children while you insert the next object or picture. For the first Long "E" variation, you will need a key, bee, tree, number 3, pea, ski, and letter "B".

What's inside the pocket?
Can you guess what you will see?
It's small and flat and unlocks doors,
Look! It's a _____ *(key).*

What's inside the pocket?
Can you guess what you will see?
It's small with wings and buzzes by,
Look! It's a _____ *(bee).*

What's inside the pocket?
Can you guess what you will see?
It's tall with branches spreading out,
Look! It's a _____ *(tree).*

What's inside the pocket?
Can you guess what you will see?
It's the number that follows number two,
Look! It's a _____ *("3").*

What's inside the pocket?
Can you guess what you will see?
It's a little round vegetable that grows in a pod,
Look! It's a _____ *(pea).*

What's inside the pocket?
Can you guess what you will see?
It's long and flat for winter fun,
Look! It's a _____ *(ski).*

What's inside the pocket?
Can you guess what you will see?
It follows in the alphabet after letter "A",
Look! It's a _____ *("B").*

Find pictures and write clues for can, man, van, pan, band, hand, and sand to try on other days. Example:

What's inside the pocket?
Guess it if you can.
It makes the hot air nice and cool,
Look! It's a _____ *(fan).*

To emphasize the long "U" sound, find pictures and write clues for glue, shoe, pew, two, zoo, "Q", "U". Example:

What's inside the pocket?
Can you guess it with a clue?
It's the color of a cloudless sky,
Look! It's the color _____ *(blue).*

I'll Tell! I'll Pass It Along

All children sit in a circle. Ask, "Who has something in your pocket?" (Have things in your pockets just in case no one has anything that day.) When someone raises his/her hand, say, "Don't tell us out loud what it is. Whisper what you have to the person next to you, who will whisper to the next person, until we get all the way back to the last person who will say it out loud. Let's see if we can listen and whisper carefully so we can all find out what is in the pocket!"

Keep a record of how many times the last person correctly named what was in the pocket. Is the group improving?

Pick A Pocket

Required materials: Several small objects with distinct characteristics, such as a red square block, a silver metal wrench, a round blue ball, or an orange carrot. Prepare a pocket board (p. 115), or an apron or shirt with several pockets.

Set up the game by placing different objects in several pockets. If your pocket space is limited, secretly replace objects that have already been used. The purpose of this language development/critical thinking game is for a child to select a pocket, take out an object, and tell the rest of the group about the object in as much detail as possible. Begin with everyone reciting this chant:

Pick a pocket, tell about it, pick a pocket now!

The first child takes out an object from a pocket and describes it. Example: "This is a red block. It is square. It is not as heavy as an apple. I like it because I can build with it." Everyone claps for the child, and the chant is repeated for the next child.

Ask children to include their feelings or opinions about the object, using the word "because". Try to include all senses and use comparisons to other objects whenever possible. Less verbal children will need prompting with questions: "Tell us what it is," or "How do you like it?" Shy children may need plenty of support, but they will feel greatly encouraged when other children model fearless responses and when they have successfully taken a turn.

Options:

1. Include classification skills by asking the child to place the object he has described in a particular category, such as living things or non-living things, or sort by color, shape, or phonetic qualities, whatever you are currently emphasizing.

2. If you are working on a particular theme or unit, select objects that enhance and complement it, such as objects that start with the letter "B" or things that belong in the water.
3. Try blindfolding the child and requiring him to describe the object through touch and smell.
4. When each child has taken a turn, set all the objects out in a row and tell a story about them, with each child contributing a part of the story. Start the story off by saying something like, "One day, a boy named Henry and a girl named Mary Beth went walking in the park. Suddenly they saw a small red block. Then..." Pause and choose a child to add the next sentence, until all the objects have been included in the story. Tape record and play it back. Some children may wish to draw pictures of the story.
5. Avoid monotony by varying the tempo, volume, and tone of the chant. Say, "This time, let's squeak like a mouse," or "Let's say it super slowly this time."

Square Like a Pocket - CPK

Square like a pocket,
Square like a frame.
Square like a pocket,
Can you say your name?
What do you like to put in your pockets?

Options:
1. Each child draws a square in the air or on the floor while the whole group recites the rhyme, repeating the rhyme several times until every child has been recognized. Vary the volume and tempo to avoid monotony.
2. Change line 4 to: "Can you clap your name?" Clap once for each syllable. Use first, middle, and last names for extra practice. When everyone has had a turn, clap some names and challenge the children to guess whose name you clapped.
3. When all the children have said their names and identified something that they like, go around the group remembering each child's name and favorite thing. Say, "Let's see if we can all remember everyone's name and the thing that they liked. Let's start with Jerome." Point to Jerome and say together, "Jerome ...candy. Sally ...rubber bands." etc. until all children are reviewed. Pause and let the children fill in the answers. This is an excellent sequential memory exercise, but also helps the children to feel smart and valued for their individual contributions.

Pocket Charades

Required materials: Picture cards of animals or objects that can easily be acted out, (perhaps those featured in a recent story, the game "What's Inside The Pocket?" or extracted from lessons in the classroom), a multi-pocket board, or an apron or shirt with several pockets.

Prepare the game by selecting and placing different picture cards in several pockets. If your pocket space is limited, keep a stack of cards with you to simply replace cards that have been chosen. The purpose of the game is for a child to pick a card, act it out for the group, and for the group to guess what it is. Begin by practicing together as a group.

A child picks a card, tells the group what it is, and then the teacher asks, "What is special about this animal?" Suppose it is a fish. Answers might be that it swims under water and blows bubbles. So the whole group pretends to swim under water and blow bubbles. Group charades may be enough of a challenge for some groups, but others will want to advance to individuals choosing cards and acting out the characteristics.

Options:

1. If you have sets of matching picture cards (as in the board game "Memory"), pocket one and display the matching pairs off to the side, so that the children can look at possible answers while they are guessing.
2. If you are featuring animals from a picture story book, display the book and page through it if the children need a hint.
3. You may want to select only three or four animals and use the same cards over and over. Each child will act them out slightly differently.
4. If children are reluctant to act out the animals, do it for them, letting them be the guessers. Be happy, confident, and a little silly and the children will join in.
5. Allow sounds for the first attempts, but as children become more skilled, use actions only.

Pocket Pass

Required materials: One portable pocket (p. 122), rhythm sticks or a drum, portable pockets for all (optional).

All children sit in a circle on the floor. Everyone chants the words illustrated at right. On the words "one" and "two", all tap the floor. The child with the portable pocket passes it on the word "pass" and the next child takes it on the word "take". Children who do not have the pocket lock their hands together on their laps during the passing and taking. Taps should be heard only on the words "one" and "two".

The chant is repeated until the pocket circulates around the entire circle. The purpose is to keep a steady, non-stop rhythm going. It is often helpful for someone to play a drum or rhythm sticks during the tapping beats. Begin very slowly at first, gradually building up speed. Again, *no stopping* is the goal. Caution your group against throwing instead of passing. Be sure to model the proper way to pass politely. This is an excellent sensory integration activity involving acute listening skills, body control, spatial relations, and eye-hand coordination.

Options:

1. Gradually introduce more pockets, until all children have them and are passing and taking simultaneously. Begin very slowly.
2. Observe whether your children cross their midlines to pass, or if they pass by shifting from hand to hand. Encourage crossing midlines by asking all children to sit on their right (or left) hands during the entire activity. Try switching directions.
3. Play background music with a matching beat and tempo, so that the game becomes a rhythmic hand dance. Whisper or mouth the chant.
4. Put several pieces of wrapped candy (or pennies, tokens, stickers, etc.) in the portable pocket. When the group has passed the pocket around without stopping, repeat and let each child remove one piece instead of tapping, passing and taking as usual. Break for snack time or move onto another activity when each child has had a turn.

Pocket Guessing

Required materials: Gather a wide variety of small objects (blocks, puzzle pieces, nuts, toy animals, nails, silly noses, marbles, paper clips, etc.) and place them in a basket or box with tall enough sides that children can not easily peek inside. Have portable or pin-on pockets on hand for those children who are not wearing pockets that day.

An effective lead-in to this game is the poem on page 11, "Put a Secret In Your Pocket." Read the poem, then ask a child to come up and select one item from the basket using his fingers only (he should not see the rest of the items or he will know what they are when other children pick them). Let him look at it and then quickly put it into his pocket. Then everyone chants:

(Name) has a secret and I wonder what it is!

Then ask him to give clues by completing these teacher read sentences:

1. The shape of my secret is *(child's answer)*.
2. The color of my secret is____________.
3. My secret is used for_______________.
4. My secret rhymes with______________.

If no one has guessed it yet, ask him to take it out to show to the group and let the next child come up and select an item. Depending on the number of objects you have, you can either put the used ones to the side, or put them back into the basket. Turn your backs to the group during the selection process if it helps to maintain the secrecy.

Pocket Same and Different

Required materials: Gather a wide variety of small objects or teaching materials (blocks, puzzle pieces, nuts, toy animals, nails, marbles, paper clips, "Memory" cards, etc.) and arrange them in pairs, with some pairs containing two identical objects. Also have a pocket board (see p. 115) or multipocket apron (see p. 121) available.

Before the children arrive, place a pair of objects in each pocket of the pocket board or apron. Take a pair out and say, "Look at these two blocks. They are the same size. They are the same color. They are the same shape. They are the same."

Then take out a mismatched pair. Say, "But look at these two buttons. They are both yellow, but one is a round button and the other one is a square button. They have the same color, they are both buttons, and they are both small, but they have different shapes, so they are not the same. These buttons are different."

Replenish the pockets and ask a child to come up and take the items from a pocket of their choice. Ask them to tell whether the objects are the same or different. Ask them to include size, shape, and color in their explanations.

For older children, include texture as a differentiating characteristic. Rough, smooth, sticky, notched, and scratched are ways to alter the texture of one of an otherwise matching pair.

Options:

1. Say, "Close your eyes and imagine a world where everything and everyone looks exactly the same. We all wear the same clothes. We all have the same hair. We are all girls or we are all boys. We all have the same moms and dads. We all have the same toys. All the houses and streets and cars and buildings look exactly alike. Everything and everyone is the same. Now open your eyes and look around. Are you glad that most things have differences, or would you rather have things be the same? How do differences help you find your way?"

Skip to My Lou

an adaptation of the Southern U. S. folksong

Lost my pocket, what'll I do?
Lost my pocket, what'll I do?
Lost my pocket, what'll I do?
Skip to my Lou, my darling.

I'll get another one, that's what I'll do,
I'll get another one, that's what I'll do,
I'll get another one, that's what I'll do,
Skip to my Lou, my darling.

Holding hands and around we go,
Holding hands and around we go,
Holding hands and around we go,
Skip to my Lou, my darling.

verse 1: All children drop their old fashioned pockets (see pattern on p. 120) or portable pockets (p. 122) inside a circle of singing children. Open hands in a helpless gesture and sway to the music.
verse 2: All children scurry to the center and select a new pocket, returning to their same place in the circle. Wave the pockets, as though to show off the new ones.
verse 3: Hold hands and circle round.

Options:

1. Provide more structure by placing a large basket in the center to hold the pockets. If the group is too excitable to select new pockets together, repeat verse 2 until all children have had a turn, one at a time.
2. Fill the pockets with take-home surprises.
3. Recite the poem, "Lucy Locket" (page 34) and tell the children about how pockets used to be bags that were carried or dangled, rather than sewn into clothing as their pockets are now is now (see pocket history on pages 8 - 10).
4. Sing the song, "Where oh where has my pocket gone?" on page 55.

Looby Loo - traditional U. S. folksong

Chorus: Here we go looby loo,
Here we go looby light,
Here we go looby loo,
All on a Saturday night.

1. I put my left hand in,
   (With your back to your group, put your left hand into a real or imaginary pocket on your left hip.)
   I put my left hand out.
   I give my hand a shake, shake, shake,
   And turn myself about.
   Chorus
2. I put my right hand in,
   (With your back to your group, put your right hand into a real or imaginary pocket on your right hip.)
   I put my right hand out.
   I give my hand a shake, shake, shake,
   And turn myself about.
   Chorus

Next, ask the children to offer ideas about what they might like to put into their pockets, and sing the next verses according to their suggestions: "I put my feather in... I put my toy in... I put my dinosaur in... " *If you have a small group, give everyone a chance. For larger groups, combine answers by putting two or three things in at once:*

3. I put my marble and my rock and my dog in,
   I put my marble and my rock and my dog out,
   I give my marble and my rock and my dog a shake, shake, shake,
   And turn myself about.
   Chorus

Ring - a - Ring - a - Roses

traditional nursery rhyme

Ring-a-ring-a-roses,
A pocket full of posies;
Ashes! Ashes!
We all fall down.

Ring-a-ring-a-roses,
A pocket full of children's idea,
Ashes! Ashes!
We all fall down.

Options:

1. Substitute *We all sit down* or *We put them down* for excitable groups that become too stimulated with the idea of "falling down." Repeat as many times as the children have ideas for.
2. Use as a simple circle dance with one large group or several smaller groups of three or four. Some children are reluctant to hold hands, so allow them to simply walk along instead. Rotate directions with each verse, saying, "Raise your right hand. Now this time, walk to the right. Jimmy, get ready with your idea for what to put in the pocket," or "Lift your left foot. Now this time, walk to the left. Jessica, get ready..."
3. Have the children remain seated and let their fingers do the dancing, forming rings with their hands and drifting them down to the floor at the end.

Sources for more learning activities using pockets:

Cooper, David & Taylor, Lynn, *Pockets*, self-published, P. O. Box 3143, Livermore, CA 94550. This is one of sixteen different themes in a series called "The Pocket Book." Each theme can be stored in a three-ring binder. Grades K-2.

Cotton, Anne; Martin, Fran; & Hope, Lyn, *Hats, Pockets, and Shoes,* Teaching Resource Center, San Leandro, CA. This is a unit from the series, "A Treasury of Themes." It contains many activities centered on clothing. Grades K-2.

Pocket Tricks That Simply Amaze

All of these pocket tricks are easy and fun. Some of them require a little preparation or practice, but you will be more than amply rewarded by the wondrous exclamations of your young audiences!

Handkerchief From An Empty Pocket

Required materials: 2 handkerchiefs and pants with deep side pockets.

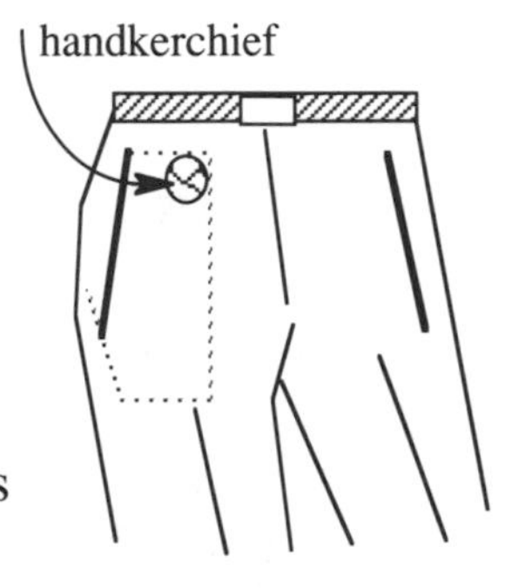

Prepare ahead by tightly wadding up the handkerchiefs and pushing them into the upper inner corners of your pants pockets, as shown in the illustration to the right. This is quite a large space, and when the pocket is pulled out, whatever is in that space remains hidden as long as it is forced tightly into the corner.

Say, "I would like to tell you the next story, but first, I need a big, white handkerchief. Does anyone have one?" Most likely, no one will... what child carries a big white handkerchief around with them? (If you don't have a *white* handkerchief, simply ask for whatever color you happen to have wadded up in your pockets.)

Next say, "Well perhaps I have one somewhere."

Make a show of searching under your chair, up your pant leg, under your shoes, under your arm pits... and finally pull out your right pants pocket to show that it is empty. Then pull out your left pants pocket to prove that it is also empty. Leave the pockets hanging out. At last, give up the search, saying, "Well, I guess I don't have one after all. We'll just have to get a magic handkerchief."

Say some "magic" words, push the right pocket back into

your pants, pretend to dig deeply inside your pocket, and immediately withdraw a large white handkerchief. Repeat the trick by saying that it would be nice to have another one. Have the children repeat the "magic" words with you, push the left pocket back into your pants, pretend to dig deeply, and pull out the other handkerchief.

Use the handkerchiefs as a prop for your next story, or simply tie the corners together to form a pouch for more pocket activities.

Button, Button, Where Is The Button?

Required materials: a large button and clothing with back pockets.

Say, "Let's play a guessing game. This is my right hand. This is my left hand. And this is my favorite button. I'm going to put my hands behind my back and put the button into one of them. I want you to guess which hand is holding the button."

When you put your hands behind your back, slip the button into your back pocket. Bring your hands around for guessing. Open your empty hand to show that the guess was wrong, then put them both behind you again, pretending to switch the button from hand to hand. After a few tries, say, "I'm only going to give you two more guesses. I have a feeling that this time, you are going to be right!"

Retrieve the button from your back pocket and put it into one of your hands. If the children guess it, the game is over. If not, show that the hand is empty, keep your hands in front, and they will use their final guess on the other hand.

Use the button for a prop for your next story, or simply go on to more right/left activities.

Disappearing Button

Required materials: thin black thread about 14" long, 2 identical small black buttons, a small safety pin, black pants with side pockets, and a cloth napkin or handkerchief.

Pull the single strand of thread through one of the buttons so that it meets evenly at one end, make a knot, and tie the knot to the safety pin, leaving about 7" of thread between the button and the pin. Attach the pin to your pants, out of sight, just inside the opening to your pocket. Hide the other button in your other pocket.

Hold the button in the palm of your hand on the same side it is attached, so the connecting thread runs between your fingers, under your hand, and out of sight into the pocket. Hold the handkerchief in your other hand.

Say, "Hey everyone! Look at this little black button. Can you see it? It may look like just a regular, old, plain button, but it's really an amazing *disappearing* button! Do you want to see it disappear? Watch this!"

Cover the button with the handkerchief. As soon as it is covered, let the button fall through your fingers and hang from the thread. With your other hand, bunch up the handkerchief in the center as though you were picking up the button underneath, remove your button hand, and fold the handkerchief a few times, finally wadding it up into a ball. Pretend to do this very carefully so that the button won't drop out. Never take your eyes away from the handkerchief. The audience should believe that the button is still in there.

Say, "Now, I will try to make the button disappear." Say some "magic" words, wave your hand, and say, "Go away, button!"

Ask one of the children to come forward and stand beside you. Give the folded handkerchief to your helper. As he unwraps it to look for the button and all the children are distracted by watching, turn away slightly and slip the hanging button into your pocket, safely out of sight. When the button can not be found, shake out the handkerchief with one hand and slip your other hand into your other pocket to retrieve the extra button. Close your fingers around it so that it is entirely hidden.

Say, "I wonder where that button could have gone?" Go up to another child and discover it behind his shirt collar (or in his ear, or hair). Show the extra button to the group. "This naughty button! I hope it stays put for a while now!"

The Magic Knot

Required materials: a rope about one foot long, a square handkerchief or scarf, and side pockets in your clothing.

Tie a loose knot into one corner of a handkerchief or scarf. Put it into your pocket with the knot on top, where you can feel it when you reach inside. Ask, "You all know what a knot is, don't you?" If some of the children appear puzzled, demonstrate and explain by tying a knot into the piece of rope. Toss it aside, then say, "Do you think that a knot can tie itself?"

When the children say that they don't think so, ask to borrow a handkerchief or a scarf. Most likely, no one will have one, but before anyone tries to give you one, put both hands in your pockets and make a show of digging for one. Finally you say, "Never mind. I found one."

Hold the knot secretly in your hand as you bring out your handkerchief. Keep the *back* of your hand toward the audience at all times, so that they don't see the knot. Let the rest of the untied handkerchief hang down. With your other hand, take one of the loose, untied corners that is hanging down and bring it up so you can hold it with the first two fingers of the same hand that is hiding the knot. Say some "magic" words, shake your hand up and down, and let go of the untied corner so that it flips back down. Look at the untied corner and appear embarrassed. Say, "Oops... those must not have been the right magic words. There's no knot in the scarf. I'd better try again."

Try again, changing your "magic" words. Again, no knot.

By this time, the children are enjoying your embarrassment and will be distracted from looking too closely at your hand. Say, "Oh! I know which magic word we forgot to say! Please! Will you all help me by saying please?"

On the third try, take the hanging corner in your fingers again, and jerk it just the way you did before. But this time, let go of the knot and hold onto the untied corner between your fingers. The hidden corner knot will flip down, and now the scarf has knotted itself!

Fee, Fie, Foe, Fum

Use this simple, traditional fingerplay to show your children how they can make something disappear, too. They will love to practice on everyone they see.

Hang your fingers and thumb out of the front of a pocket. Just stick them back in to make them disappear. Ask all the children to do it with you. If they aren't wearing pockets, have them make their fingers disappear by putting them behind their backs.

Fee, fie, foe, fum,
See my fingers?
See my thumb?
Fee, fie, foe, fum,
Finger's gone,
So is thumb!

Disappearing Coin

Required materials: one 5” square of unfolded paper, a quarter, a handkerchief or scarf, and pants with side pockets in them.

In this trick, you fold a secret pocket with the paper, and then secretly hide the coin in your real pocket. Say, “Would you like to see me make this quarter disappear? But I can’t do it by myself. I need the help of this magical piece of paper.”

1. Place the square on a flat surface and put the quarter in the middle. Fold the bottom edge *almost* to the top edge, leaving one half inch on top.

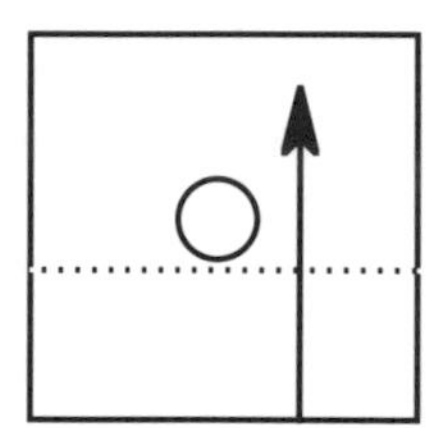

2. Fold both layers of the right side under and crease on the dotted line.

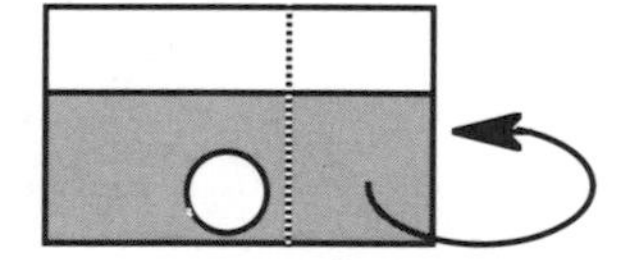

3. Fold both layers of the left side under (this side will overlap the right side on the back) and crease on the dotted line.

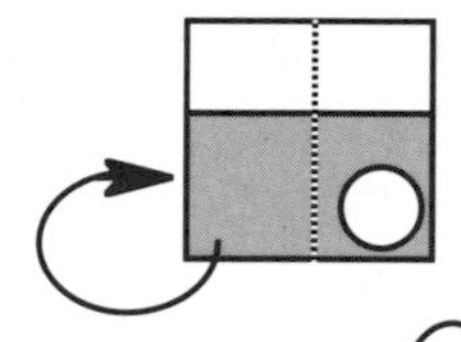

4. Fold back the half inch flap on top so that it covers the two overlapping sides in back.

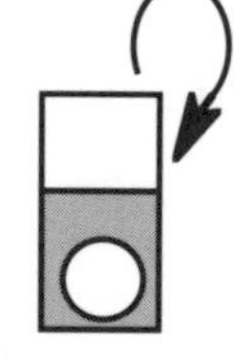

The quarter is securely folded inside the paper. Do not let the children observe the secret opening.

Let the children feel the quarter through the paper. When they have all agreed that the quarter is wrapped tightly inside, return to your place in front. But as you walk back, quickly turn the paper pocket upside down and let the quarter slide out of the secret opening into your hand. Slip the quarter into your pants pocket while you distract the children by waving the magic handkerchief. Now that the quarter has safely disappeared, place the paper pocket on the table, cover it with the magic handkerchief, say some "magic" words, and ask one of the children to come up and check to see if the coin has disappeared.

While all the children are watching your helper unfold the paper, secretly withdraw the quarter from your pants pocket, walk to the edge of the group, and when your helper announces that the quarter is missing, you can mysteriously "find" it in one of the other children's hair, collar, or ear.

Sing "In A Pocket Clemintine" (p. 58) which features coins, then go on to other money identification activities.

Hickory Dickory Docket
A Mouse Wants In The Pocket

Required materials: a stuffed toy mouse (you can find these in the pet section of discount stores - they are cat toys), 1 strand of black thread about 12 inches long, 1 safety pin, and a dark colored shirt with an upper pocket in it.

Tie a knot in one end of the single strand of thread and sew it through the mouse's nose, then tie the other end to the safety pin. Attach the pin to your shirt, just inside the pocket opening so that it doesn't show. Pull the mouse out of your pocket and say, "Look who was hiding in my pocket! Oh no! I think he's trying to get back in there!"

Hold out the mouse on one palm and put the other palm a few inches in front of it. As you move the hand holding the mouse away from your body, the mouse will appear to jump into your other hand. Keep moving your hands, and it will look as if it is trying to get back into your pocket.

Recite the pocketized rhyme "Hickory Dickory Docket" on page 34. Follow with other fingerplays about mice (page 21) or hamsters (pages 83-88), or read the picture story books, *The Pocket Mouse* and *Two in a Pocket* (sources on pages 49-50).

Hamsters - Marsupials - Pelicans

Activities About Animals With Natural Pockets

Did you know that...

Hamster pouches are stretchy bags of skin that reach from the face to the shoulders. They are noticeable, even when empty. Food or bedding are carried in the pouches, and even small babies are carried in times of danger. Hamsters make fine pets, but in the wild, they live in burrows and come from the Middle East. They are most active at night and eat both plants and tiny animals.

Hamster Pockets - CPK

I think it's kind of funny
That hamsters oh so small,
Can shovel in the food they do
Without a spoon at all.

The pockets all around their face
Never seem to fill.
Scooping up the seeds they like,
Their hands are rarely still.

I wish my cheeks had pockets
To store the things I like.
I'd put in pizza, fruit, and toys,
And maybe my brand new bike.

I think it's kind of funny
That hamsters oh so small
Can stuff so much in pockets
Without splitting seams at all.

Ten Fat Hamsters - CPK

Ten fat hamsters in a pocket nest,
One grew, two grew, so did all the rest.
They ate and ate and grew and grew;
They simply would not stop
Until one day they ate too much
and the pocket just went... POP!

Options:

1. Blow up a lightweight plastic bag after the words *grew* and *ate*. Be ready to pop the bag on the word *POP!* Pass out paper lunch bags for everyone to try, but don't be surprised if the youngest children can't hold theirs closed. Instead, let them pop your bag.
2. Try filling cheeks with air and then blowing the air out on the word *POP!*

Hamster Is Hiding - CPK

My hamster is hiding, but where oh where?
Under the table? Under the chair?
I look and look for her everywhere.
When I stop searching and finally say,
"Here Hamster, here's some food."
She pops out of my pocket right away!

Options:

1. Ask, "If you were a hamster, where would you hide? Why would you want to hide? Would you want to be found?"
2. This rhyme is an excellent lead-in to several of the picture storybooks listed on page 87. Many of them feature lost or escaped hamsters.

?

Why does a hamster have such a short neck?
Because his head is so close to his body.

Rattle and squeak, hamsters make something
that no one can see. Can you guess what it is?
Noise!

Ten Little Hamsters - CPK

Let each of your fingers represent a hamster.

Ten little hamsters were living in a school,
This one said, "Let's sleep where it's cool."
This one said, "It's early in the day."
This one said, "Come on, let's play."
This one said, "I'm hungry as can be."
This one said, "There's a carrot for me."
This one said, "Wait, we'd better look."
This one said, "Yes, it's under a book."
This one said, "Can't we get it anyway?"
This one said, "I think we may."
This one said, "Let's push the book away."
So they all helped out and ate all day.

Little Hamster - CPK

See the little hamster
Creeping up the stair,
*(Creep your hand up your leg
to your lower pants pocket.)*
Looking for a warm nest.
There - Oh! There!
(*Put your hand in your pocket.)*

?

What is it that every hamster in the whole
world is doing at the same time?
Growing older.

Why does a hamster go to bed?
Because the bed won't come to him.

What smells most in the hamster's cage?
The hamster's nose.

The Hole In My Pocket - CPK

(sing to the tune of "On Top Of Old Smoky")

The hole in my pocket,
I'm sorry to say,
Let loose my pet hamster,
It wiggled away.

It crawled down my pant leg
And unto my shoe,
And then my pet hamster
Knew just what to do.

It ran from my bedroom,
And straight down the hall,
And then my pet hamster,
It had a big fall.

It fell down the first step,
And then all the rest,
And then my pet hamster,
It found a new nest.

For there at the bottom,
Was mother's new shoe,
A new home for hamster,
The cage would not do.

The hole in my pocket,
I'm sorry to say,
Is still big as ever,
It won't go away!

Options:

1. Sing the song and ask the children to clap (play an instrument, stand up, raise their hands, etc.) only when they hear the word *hamster*.
2. Tell the story, "The Pocket Holes Of Pocketville" (p. 43) or read Marci Ridlon's poem, "Hamsters", (source on p. 88). Try the trick, "Hickory Dickory Docket" (p. 81) or sing songs about pocket holes (p. 54 & 61).
3. Ask, "Who has a hamster at home? Has it ever escaped? Where did you find it?" This is a good lead-in to a discussion about pet care and the responsibilities involved in having a pet.

Where do hamsters go on their second birthday?
Into their third year.

?

Picture storybooks about hamsters

*Indicates especially wonderful!

Ambrus, Victor, ***Grandma, Felix, and Mustapha Biscuit***, 1982, William Morrow and Co., New York, NY. Felix the cat tries to capture Mustapha the hamster, but only succeeds in getting himself into trouble. Pockets are seen on the Grandma's apron, but mostly this is a funny hamster story.

Baker, Alan, ***Benjamin's Portrait***, 1986, Lothrop, Lee & Shepard Books, New York, NY. Benjamin hamster works on a self-portrait, eventually overcoming mishaps and imperfection. Other books by Alan Baker about this hamster character are: ***Benjamin and the Box, Benjamin's Balloon, Benjamin Bounces Back, Benjamin's Dreadful Dream, and Benjamin's Book.***

Blacker, Terence, (ill. Pippa Unwin),** ***Herbie Hamster, Where Are You?, 1990, Random House, New York, NY. Danny hunts for Herbie throughout his neighborhood, finally finding him and bringing him home in his pocket. The illustrations provide rich details of the various life styles of the people in his neighborhood, as well as hide Herbie in each picture.

Brandenberg, Franz, (ill. Aliki), ***The Hit Of The Party***, 1985, Greenwillow Books, New York, NY. Jim and Kate are going to a costume party, but first Jim has to feed Cheeks, his hamster. The hamster escapes and is finally found in the feathers of his costume.

Brook, Judy, ***Hector & Harriet: The Night Hamsters***, 1984, Andre Deutsch, London. Two stories about the nightly adventures of two escaped hamsters. In the first story, the hamsters frighten away a dog and cat. In the second, they frighten away people who can't understand how a variety of musical instruments can play by themselves. Nothing specifically about pockets, but good hamster stories.

Murschetz, Luis, *A Hamster's Journey*, 1975, Prentice-Hall, Inc., Engelwood Cliffs, NJ. Wheeler the hamster rolls out of his cage in his running wheel. All the other hamsters in the city come to his rescue in their running wheels, forming an armada of hamster wheels rolling down the highway. They finally stop in a wheat field where they discard their wheels and learn to live in the wild. Nothing specifically about pockets, but this is a hilarious hamster adventure.

Prelutsky, Jack, (Ill. Marc Brown), *Read-Aloud Rhymes For The Very Young*, 1989, Alfred A. Knopf, New York. A poem on page 54 by Marci Ridlon, "Hamsters" ends with the lines "...and they sit inside your pocket when you are all alone." This poem also appears in Marci Ridlon's, *That Was Summer*, 1969, Follett Publishing Co.

Vaes, Alain, *The Wild Hamster*, 1985, Little, Brown and Co., Boston, MA. A strange tale about a hamster that eats so much that it eventually grows to the size of an elephant. At last it is captured and put to work turning the wheel at the mill, which is why hamsters still enjoy having wheels in their cages. Lovely illustrations.

Wolcott, Patty, (ill. Rosekrans Hoffman), *Where Did That Naughty Little Hamster Go?, 1974, J. B. Lippincott, New York, NY. Children hunt everywhere throughout a classroom until their hamster is finally found.

Non-fiction books about hamsters

Anders, Rebecca, *Winslow the Hamster*, 1977, Carolrhoda Books, Minneapolis, MN. Hunting for sunflower seeds in pockets is part of the text on the first page. A good photo of hamsters' pouches is included.

Watts, Barrie, *Hamster*, 1986, Silver Burdett Co., Morristown, NJ. Simple factual text describes hamsters in full detail and includes large colored photographs. An especially fine photograph of the hamster's full cheek pouches is found on p. 17.

Marsupials

Kangaroos, koalas, and opossums all belong to the marsupial family. All female marsupials have pouches on their bellies where immature babies feed and develop after birth. Kangaroo babies, called joeys, are only the size of a lima bean at birth. They crawl to the safety of their mother's pouch where they develop for about eight more months, finally popping out to explore the world. They continue to use their mother's pouch as a resting place or place of safety for several more months. Only female marsupials have pockets.

Little Joey - CPK

Start with your hand in your pocket.
Little Joey lives in a hole
So dry and cozy down below.
He pops his ears up *(stick up two fingers)*, then his nose,
Big hind legs and away he goes.
Bye mom! See you later!
Hoppity, hoppity, hoppity!

Kangaroo Limerick - CPK

There once was a kangaroo funny
Who hopped all around like a bunny.
With a pocket so wide,
Her baby could ride,
In the rain or when it was sunny.

Who can hop around quickly, without touching the ground?
A baby kangaroo riding in his mommy's pocket!

Little Kanga - CPK

There was a little kangaroo,
Who was always on the jump.
He never looked ahead,
So he always got a bump.
He'd hide inside Mom's pocket
'Til the ouchy went away,
Then he'd pop outside again
To hop and leap and play.

Pouch Poke Ouch Grouch - CPK

Keep your hands to yourself
Near a marsupial's pouch.
One little poke
Brings an, "Ouch, ouch, ouch!"
Deep inside the baby hides
Poking always hurts his sides.
So don't you forget...
Keep your hands to yourself
Near marsupial's pouch.
Or you'll quickly find out
Who's a great big GROUCH!
Pouch!
Poke!
Ouch!
Grouch!
Oh, oh...Run for it!

?

What kind of bush does a kangaroo
sit under in the rain?
A wet one!

Did you hear about the two kangaroos that got
married and lived *hoppily* ever after?

Possum Opossum - CPK

Possum opossum lives in a tree.
(Raise arms for tall branches.)
She hangs by her tail and has babies three.
(Hold up three fingers.)

She carries them safely upon her back.
(Move three fingers to your back.)
All around town like a peddler's pack.
(Pretend to hold a heavy bag.)

Possum opossum pretends to die.
(Close eyes.)
When red fox pounces, so still she does lie.
(Put head on hands as though asleep.)

A marsupial with a pocket built in
(Slip hands into your pockets.)
Possum opossum is kangaroo kin!

Make-a-kanga - CPK

Can you make a kangaroo
With two ears straight up high?
(Pointer and middle fingers up.)
A pouch in front to hold the babe
(Thumb holding ring finger down, forming a circular hole.)
Now hop up to the sky.
Boing! Boing! Boing! Boing!
Up and down like a spring.
Boing! Boing! Boing! Boing!
Please, where're you going?
To the grass, fresh and sweet?
Now it's time to stop and eat.
Munch.

Possums, koalas, kangaroos - CPK

Possums, koalas, kangaroos,
Marsupials all, here are the clues:
Mamas with pouches,
Covered with hair,
Babies drink milk,
From deep inside there.
Possums in trees, koalas too,
Hopping on grass is the kangaroo.
Possums, koalas, kangaroos,
Marsupials all, which do you choose?

Required materials for a marsupial matching game: 3 shoe boxes, several cut-outs of koalas, kangaroos, and opossums (patterns on p. 94 - 95), 2 pictures of trees, one picture of green grass, and an apron with a wide front pouch pocket.

Set up: Staple a tree and an opossum to one box and place it close to the children to represent the opossum's home (a North American tree-loving animal). Staple the other tree and a koala to the second box and place it further away to represent the koala's home (an Australian tree-loving animal). And finally, staple a kangaroo and the picture of grass to the third box, placing it next to the koala's box, representing the kangaroo's home on the grassy Australian plains. Cut out several koalas, kangaroos, and opossums and write the following facts on the backs (one fact per cut-out):

Kangaroos:
1. Eats grass.
2. Hops fast.
3. Babies are called joeys.
4. Lives in Australia, far away.
5. Has a long, strong tail.

Koalas:
1. Eats leaves.
2. Moves slowly.
3. Lives in trees.
4. Has round ears.
5. Lives in Australia, far away.

Opossums:

1. Eats almost anything, including garbage.
2. Has a long skinny tail.
3. Lives in trees.
4. Lives in North America, close by.
5. Pretends to be dead when it's bothered by others.

Place the cut-outs in your apron pocket (ideally a wide pouch pocket similar to a kangaroo's pouch) and describe the three boxes, naming the marsupials and telling about them. Say, "Today we are going to play a game about marsupials. Mother marsupials are animals that have pockets on their bellies, similar to this pocket *(point to your apron pocket).* There are many different kinds of marsupials, but our game only has three different kinds: kangaroos, opossums, and koalas." Use one or several of thebooks listed in the resource section to show the children what marsupials look like and a globe to show where both your home and Australia are located.

Recite the poem, asking the children to say lines 1 and 9 with you. Ask a child to come up and reach into your pocket, picking out a cut-out. Ask, "Can you name this animal?" Then read the fact on the back and ask the children to recite the fact as a group as the child places the cut-out into its proper box. Chant the last two lines of the poem for each child.

For older children, ask them to remember facts from material you have already presented.

When is a possum like ink?
When it's in a pen.

How many big koalas are born in Australia?
None - only little babies are born.

Did you hear about the angry mother kangaroo who pulled her baby out of her pocket and said, "How many times have I told you not to eat cookies in bed?"

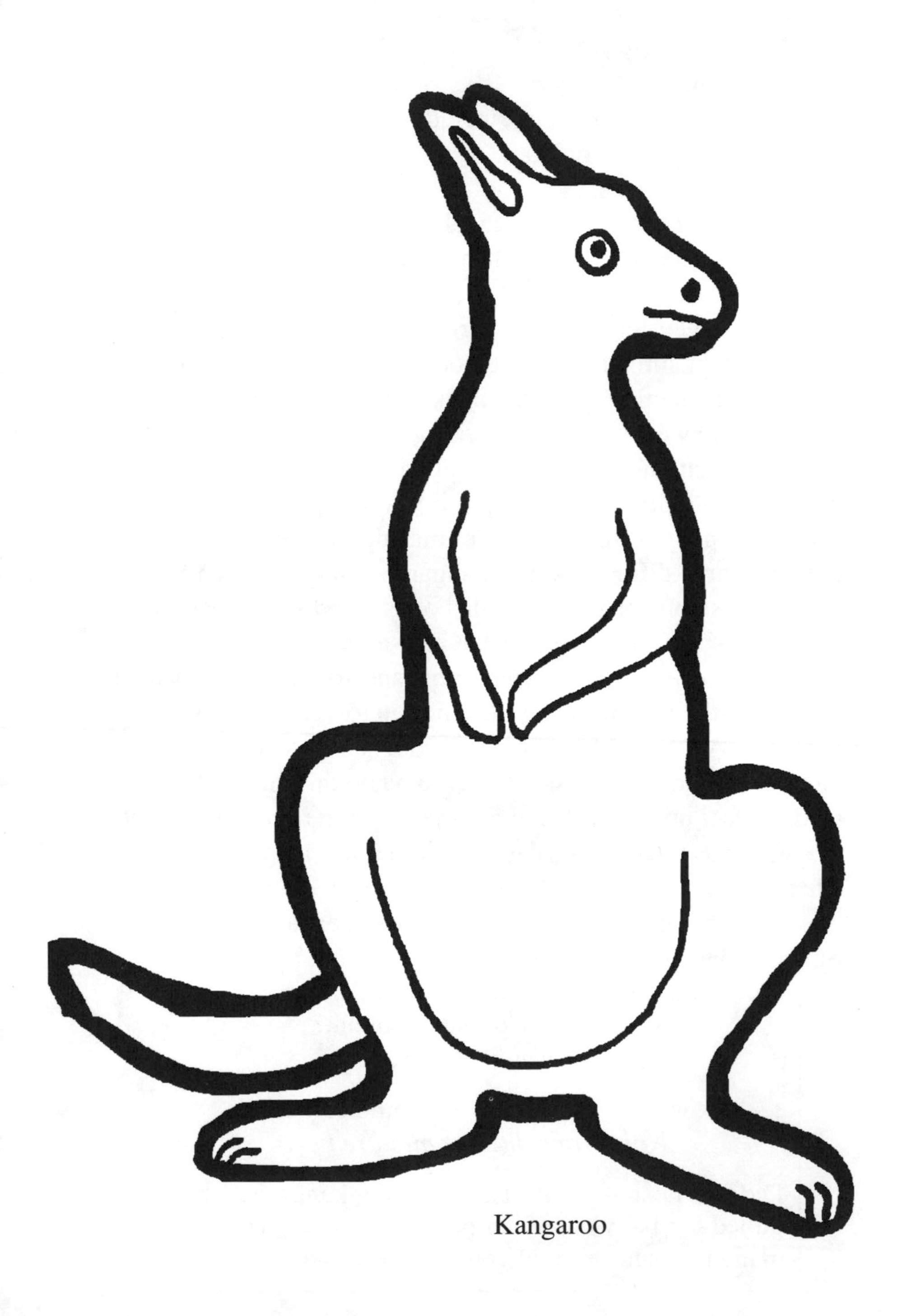

Kangaroo

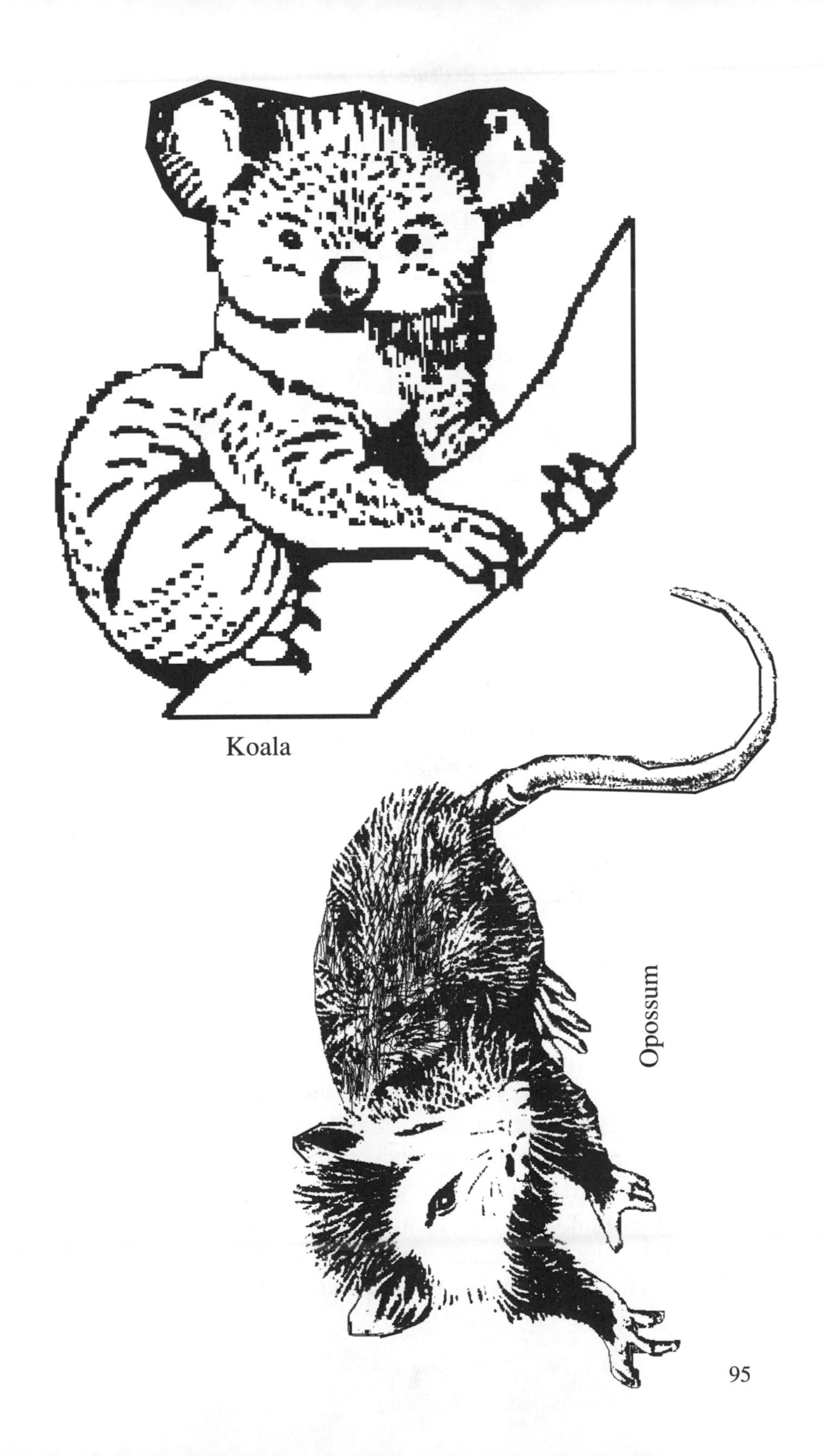

Koala

Opossum

Guess Who?
Legs like a rabbit,
Ears like a mule.
Pocket like a sweatsuit
And hops really cool.
Who is it?
A mama kangaroo!

Picture storybooks about kangaroos, koalas, and opossums

*Indicates especially wonderful!

Christelow, Eileen, *Olive and the Magic Hat, 1987, Clarion Books, New York, NY. The opossum family prepares for father's birthday, but his present, a tall black hat, falls out of the window and lands on the head of Mr. Foxley. The children go to great lengths to get it back just in time for the party. Includes a reference to pockets, but mostly it's a funny story featuring opossums.

***Du Bois, William Pene, *Bear Circus*,** 1971, The Viking Press, New York, NY. When grasshoppers eat all of the koala bears' food, kangaroo friends come to their rescue by transporting them in their pockets to find new food. The bears reward them by presenting a circus. Although the book is a bit long, the illustrations are large and humorous, and the plot has one adventure after another.

Fox, Mem, (ill. Pamela Lofts), *Koala Lou, 1988, Gulliver

Books, Harcourt Brace Jovanovich, New York, NY. Baby koala trains for the bush Olympics in order to gain her mother's attention and approval. Bright, lively illustrations capture the humor and sentiment. No mention of pockets, but a good koala story.

Fox, Mem, (ill. Julie Vivas), *Possum Magic, 1983, Gulliver Books, Harcourt Brace Jovanovich, New York, NY. Grandma Possum makes Baby Hush invisible and must travel throughout Australia sampling different foods in order to make her visible again. Includes koalas and kangaroos. No direct references to pockets, but the humorous color illustrations of the three different marsupials are large and exciting.

Guarino, Deborah, (ill. Steven Kellogg), *Is your Mama a Llama?*, 1989, Scholastic Inc., New York, NY. Lloyd the baby llama asks his different animals friends, "Is your mama a llama?" Included among the friends is a baby kangaroo, who gives Lloyd a hint about his mother's pocket.

Hamsa, Bobbie, (ill. Tom Dunnington), *Your Pet Kangaroo*, 1980, Ideals Publishing Corp., Milwaukee, WI. A humorous do's and don'ts book about the care of kangaroos, with an eight page section about fanciful uses for their pockets.

Jensen, Kiersten, (ill. Tony Oliver), *Possum in the House,* 1989, Gareth Stevens Children's Books, Milwaukee, WI. Repetitive text with large full-colored illustrations make this an excellent opossum story for very young listeners. The Australian opossum is used and it looks quite different than American types.

Keller, Holly, *Too Big*, 1983, Greenwillow Books, New York, NY. The characters are opossums, the illustrations are two color line drawings, and the story is about the introduction of a new baby to the family. It's odd that an opossum baby comes home from the hospital and not the mother's pouch, but the text is simple and very positive.

***Kent, Jack, *Joey*,** 1984, Prentice Hall, Inc., Englewood Cliffs, NJ. Joey, a young kangaroo, invites his friends over to play in his mother's pouch. All goes well until too many toys are brought in.

***Kent, Jack, *Joey Runs Away*,** 1985, Prentice Hall, Inc., Englewood Cliffs, NJ. Joey decides that it would be easier to run away from home than to clean his messy pocket. While he tries to move into a pelican and mail pouch, several animals try to move into his old room. Finally, he returns to clean his room. This story is also available on video and cassette tapes from Weston Woods, Weston, CT.

***Levenson, Dorothy (ill. Ruth Wood), *Too Many Pockets*,** 1984, Price/Stern/Sloan, Inc., Los Angeles, CA. Joey, a baby kangaroo, becomes impatient about having to wait to explore the world, so he pops out and takes off when his mother is busy eating grass. He finds other pockets to hop into, an apron, a school bag, and a mail pouch, before he returns to one of his very own. Also available as a read-along cassette to accompany the book as listed above. Narrated by Dyan Forest: *Wonderland Easy Reader, Price/Stern/Sloan, Inc. 1982, Los Angeles, CA.*

Mayer, Mercer, *What Do You Do With A Kangaroo?*, 1973, Macmillan Publishing Co., New York, NY. Unlikely large animals invade the home of a little girl who tries to throw them out and go about her day, eventually having to accept their presence. Although not necessarily about pockets, award winning illustrations make this book fun.

Pape, Donna, (ill. Tom Eaton), *The Sleep-Leaping Kangaroo*, 1973, Garrard Publishing Co., Champaign, IL. Kara Kangaroo visits several animals each night while sleep-leaping. She finally solves the problem by putting rocks in her pocket.

***Pape, Donna, (ill. Tom Eaton), *Where Is My Little Joey?*,** 1978, Garrard Publishing Co., Champaign, IL. Kara's baby leaves while she naps. During the panicky search, silly things are placed in her pocket, until a warm reunion unites them again.

Pape, Donna & Kessler, Leonard, (ill. Tom Eaton), *Play Ball, Joey Kangaroo!*, 1980, Garrard Publishing Co., Champaign, IL. Kara and Joey Kangaroo are too little to play ball with the children so Kara invents kangaroo ball to play with her cousins. Their pockets serve as baskets for the game.

Payne, Emmy, (ill. H. A. Rey), *Katy No-Pocket, 1944, Houghton Mifflin Company, Boston, MA. Katy Kangaroo is sad because she has no pocket in which to carry her son, so she investigates how other animals carry their babies. Finally, she solves her problem by getting an apron with enough pockets for her baby and all his friends. This story is also available on cassette tape from Houghton Mifflin Products: Brilliance Corp., 1989.

Schlein, Miriam, (ill. Joan Auclair), *Big Talk*, 1990, Bradbury Press, New York, NY. A baby kangaroo boasts and fantasizes about achieving great things, and then finally retires to his mother's warm pocket.

Wiseman, Bernard, (ill. Robert Lopshire), *Little New Kangaroo, 1973, Macmillan Publishing Co., Inc., New York, NY. Little New Kangaroo goes for his first ride through the Australian countryside and eventually invites four new friends (a koala bear, a bandicoot, a wombat, and a platypus) to join him in his mother's pouch (short, rhyming text).

Resources for other marsupial rhymes or stories:

Catron, Elaine and Parks, Barbara, (ill. Jane Shasky), *Super Story Telling*, 1986, T. S. Denison & Co., Minneapolis, MN. There's a rhyme on p. 15 called "Five Little Koala Bears". Includes a reproducible pattern of a koala and a eucalyptus tree.

Cromwell, Liz, (ill. Sue Yagiela Williams), ***Finger Frolics,*** 1976, Partner Press, Livonia, MI. Two fingerplays on page 62: "The Brown Kangaroo" and "The Kangaroo".

Hunt, Tamara, (Ill. Nancy Renfro), ***Pocketful of Puppets: Never Pick A Python For A Pet***, 1984, Nancy Renfro Studios, Austin, TX. Good ideas for using puppets with pocketed aprons. An especially cute activity on p.32 is about a mother and baby kangaroo puppet.

Irving, Jan and Currie, Robin, ***Raising The Roof: Children's Stories and Activities on Houses***, 1991, Teacher Ideas Press, Englewood, Co. There's an action rhyme about kangaroo pockets on page 163 called "Pocket Home".

Scott, Louise Binder, ***Rhymes For Learning Times,*** 1983, T. S. Denison & Co., Minneapolis, MN. A rhyme on p. 143, "Kangaroo" is a cute activity for practicing gross motor skills (hopping, self-control). The text also includes lines about the pouch.

Non-fiction picture books about marsupials:

Arnold, Caroline, (photo. Richard Hewett), ***Kangaroo,*** 1987, and ***Koala***, 1987, both books published by William Morrow & Co., Inc. New York. Large color photographs of kangaroos and koalas of all ages, including newborns. The text is too long for preschoolers, but the details in the photographs are very good.

Burt, Denise, (photo. Neil McLeod), ***Birth of a Koala,*** 1986, Buttercup Books, Victoria, Australia. Excellent color photographs of koalas of all ages, but the text is too long and complex for preschoolers.

Crowcroft, Peter, (ill. Colin Threadgall), ***Australian Marsupials,*** 1972, A McGraw-Hill Natural Science Picture Book, New York & San Francisco. Large color and black & white illustrations give clear and accurate information for young children. Includes informations about opossums.

Hurd, Edith Thatcher, (ill. Clement Hurd), ***The Mother Kangaroo***, 1976, Little, Brown & Co., Boston, MA. The life cycle of a kangaroo is described in short, clear, and accurate text and illustrated with two colored block prints. Of special interest is the birth process and the realistic use of the mother's pouch. This is a good source for children who want to know what *really* happens.

LaBastille, Anne, ***The Opossums***, 1973, The National Wildlife Federation, Washington, D. C. Large color photographs of opossums in natural settings as well as two short stories based on characters from the "Ranger Rick" magazine, "Zelda Possum Cleans Up" and "Look Out For Possumnappers!"

Petty, Kate,** ***Kangaroos, 1990, Gloucester Press, New York. Large color photographs and illustrations describe how a baby kangaroo is born and grows up. Simple text makes this book excellent for very young children.

Stonehouse, Bernard, ***Kangaroos***, 1977, Raintree Children's Books, Milwaukee, WI. Factual accounts of kangaroos with full colored photographs on every page. Excellent photos of newborn kangaroos with simple text explaining about the uses of the kangaroo's pocket.

Did you know that...

A pelican pouch is elastic skin that is fastened to its lower beak and neck. The pelican opens its beak underwater, spreads its enormous pouch, and scoops up almost three gallons of fish and water. On the surface, it tilts its head up, tips its beak, and allows the water to drain out. It swallows the fish while floating on the waves. Pelicans eat as much as four pounds of fish every day. Its pouch also helps keep the bird cool in summer's heat. Heat escapes from the pelican's body through the bare skin of the pouch. Although many stories are written about pelicans carrying objects in their pouches, they do not carry fish from place to place. Even when they feed their babies, pelican parents regurgitate fish they have already swallowed.

Five Brown Pelicans - CPK

Use fingers or flannel board figures to dramatize this rhyme.

Five brown pelicans sat on the shore,
One went swimming and then there were four.
Four brown pelicans looked out to sea,
One went fishing, and then there were three.
Three brown pelicans with nothing to do,
One took a dive, and then there were two.
Two brown pelicans sat in the sun,
One chased a fishing boat, and then there was one.
One lonely pelican said, "This is no fun."
He flew away, and then there were none.

When a pelican falls into the water,
what is the first thing it does?
Get wet!

What do pelicans have that no other animals have?
Little pelicans.

The Pelican - CPK

The pelican likes to swim like this,
His mouth wide open to catch a fish.
(Hold palms together with the fingers
extended like an open mouth.)
But when he sees me on the shore,
He flies away to be seen no more.
(Flap your arms.)

Built-In Net - CPK

Use the patterns on page 111 to make a pelican puppet that you can feed while you tell this poem. Make paper fish (p. 114) and tape them to heavy stones, so that the weight of the fish will stretch the nylon of the pelican's pouch. Repeat the poem, but let the children put in fish and other, less probable things.

Have you ever seen a bird
With such a stretchy bill?
It doesn't seem so big at first
Until it starts to fill.

There's room for tubs of water
And loads of wiggling fish.
A pelican just tips its head
To gulp down its tasty dish.

The pockets in my sweaters
Unlike a pelican's beak,
Won't carry fish and water
For they always spring a leak.

No drippy pockets for pelicans
Who love it where it's wet.
If they want catch a fish,
They have a built-in net!

The Pelican - *Dixon Lanier Merritt (1910)
(adapted for young children)
A wonderful bird is the pelican,
His bill will hold more than his belican *(belly can).*
He can take in his beak
Food enough for a week,
But I can't see how in the world he can.

**From The Pelican Chorus - ***Edward Lear (1877)
Ploffskin, Pluffskin, Pelican jee!
We think no birds as happy as we!
Plumpskin, Ploshkin, Pelican jill!
We thought so then, and we think so still!

*From *Bartletts Familiar Quotations 15th and 125th Anniversary Edition*, 1980, Little, Brown and Co., Boston.

Five Little Pelicans - CPK
Remove two fish props (pattern on page 114) from your pocket or simply pantomime.

Five little pelicans at a Florida key,
A father, a mother, and babies three.
(Point to your five fingers to represent the family.)
Father brought a bass,
Mother brought a trout,
Three little babies picked them out.
This one grabbed the bass,
This one grabbed the trout,
And this one whined, "Hey, I'm left out!"
No trout.
No bass.
Alas.
Better luck next time...

How Pelican Got His Pouch

A Two Minute Version of a Caribbean Folktale

Optional props: Several cut-outs of fish (p. 114), some large and some small. Put them in your pockets and pull them out whenever the birds in the story dive down to catch fish.

Three bird friends, Pelican, Frigate Bird, and Booby Bird, sat together on a rock by the sea. Two of the birds, Frigate Bird and Pelican, were fast fliers. They both had good eyesight and were good divers, but Frigate Bird was much better at catching fish. When Frigate Bird dived down into the water, he always came up with large flashing fish that were delicious to eat. But when Pelican dived down into the water, he came up with little fish that barely made a snack, and sometimes, he didn't catch any fish at all.

This would not have been a problem, except that Frigate Bird never shared his large delicious fish. And he never stopped talking about what a good fisher he was.

"I am the fastest flier. I am the best diver. I have the best eyesight. I catch the largest fish. You other birds should watch me because I am the best." Frigate bird bragged and bragged all day long.

Booby Bird, who was very clever, and Pelican, who was just as large and fast as Frigate Bird, were tired of all this bragging every day. And they were hungry, too, because all of the smaller fish had left the area and only big fish remained. Pelican and Booby bird could not catch the big fish, and Frigate Bird would not share with them.

Booby Bird said, "I think that Pelican can fly and see and dive just as well as you can, Frigate Bird. I think that if Pelican had a longer beak with a pouch like yours, he would catch even larger fish than you can catch."

Well, Frigate Bird was not happy about that idea. "What? Pelican could not possibly catch fish as well as I can, even if he had my nice long beak with the pouch on it! I am the best and I will always be the best!" said Frigate Bird.

"I don't believe you," said Booby Bird. "Why don't you trade beaks and find out?"

And so Frigate Bird gave his long beak with the pouch to Pelican, and Pelican gave his shorter beak to Frigate Bird. Just as Booby Bird had predicted, Pelican with his new long beak with the pouch could now easily catch big fish. But Frigate Bird could not catch big fish at all with Pelican's shorter beak.

The trouble was, Frigate Bird was afraid to tell his friends that he couldn't catch big fish anymore. So he pretended to catch fish and then lied about it. Frigate Bird said, "See? I told you I was the best! Even with Pelican's beak, I can still catch the biggest fish!"

Booby Bird said, "Oh, that is wonderful. I am glad that you are still such a good fisher. Now all of our problems are solved. Pelican should keep your long beak with the pouch and you should keep Pelican's shorter beak. Then we will all have plenty of big, delicious fish to eat!"

"No! No!" shouted Frigate Bird. "I want my long beak with the pouch back! Give it back to me!"

But Pelican was too busy catching fish to return Frigate Bird's beak. And today, you can still see Pelican busily diving for fish with his long beak with the pouch. And Frigate Bird? He never sits on the rock with Booby Bird and Pelican anymore. Frigate Bird flies out to sea all by himself, chasing after fishing boats and stealing fish from the fishing nets. The fishermen say that he's still trying to get his beak back, and maybe some day he will.

Options:

1. Booby Birds, or gannets, are goose-like relatives of pelicans that live in warm sea waters. Frigate Birds are large sea birds that are known for their rapid flying speeds.

2. Try telling this condensed version of a Caribbean folktale in the traditional way by beginning the tale with the statement, "Crick Crack". Listeners should then respond by saying, "Break my back." When the story is finished, say, "Wire bend" and the listeners respond by saying, "Story end."
3. Ask, "Which bird did you like best? Which bird didn't you like? Do you like to hear bragging? Why was Frigate Bird afraid to admit that he couldn't catch fish anymore? Do you think that birds can really trade beaks? Why?"

Back To The Pelicans

Optional props: Flannel board figures of a pelican, snake, egret, heron, raccoon, turtle, and alligator (see p. 112 - 114 for patterns).

Not long ago, a family made up of a dad, mom, brother, and sister took a trip to Florida to visit their grandparents. While they were there, they went to see the Florida Everglades, which is a large swampy place where lots of snakes, alligators, and birds live.

Sister said, "I wish we could go out and explore the swamp."

Brother said, "Let's rent an airboat and glide along the top of the water."

Mom and Dad said, "Well, we think that would be all right. But we'd better take a map along. It would be terrible to get lost in this strange tangled swamp."

So they rented an airboat and started the engine to drive away. The motor was so loud that they had to shout to be heard, even though they were sitting next to each other. So instead of trying to talk, they began to point and motion with their hands. As they were about to lose sight of the boat dock, Brother pointed up to the sky. Over the dock, were five large birds. They had wide wings and long heavy beaks.

"Pelicans!" shouted Mom.

Next, Sister pointed to a tall white bird standing still in the tall grasses.

"Egret!" shouted Dad.

Their pointing fingers were very busy as they rode along, the airboat roaring as it barely skimmed the surface of the dark shallow water. They saw several tall blue herons stabbing their long beaks at shellfish. They saw a dark snake with yellow stripes wound tightly around a branch that hung out over the water. They saw the ringed tail of a brown raccoon disappear as it turned to go back into the bushes. They saw many green turtles sunning themselves on fallen logs. But mostly they were searching for the cold eyes and jagged teeth of an alligator floating in the dark water.

The river through the Everglades had many turns and bends. Sometimes it was wide like a lake, and other times, the waterway was narrow and very grassy. Dad and Mom watched the map carefully, but they also kept their eyes on the sky, never losing sight of the pelicans back at the dock.

Finally, Sister's eyes got wide and she began to point frantically. There along the edge of the water, was a long bumpy black alligator taking a nap in the sun. Everyone cheered as the lazy reptile slid into the water, leaving only a couple of small bubbles behind.

"Back to the pelicans!" shouted Mom.

"Back to the pelicans!" shouted the rest of the family. They could hardly wait to tell their grandparents about everything they had seen during their Everglades adventure.

Options:

1. Pull the flannel board figures out of your pocket as you tell the story. When the story is over, ask the children to name them. Then take them away, and ask them to remember the animals from the story. Put them back up as they call out the names. Challenge them to remember the animals in the same order that they appeared in the story. Then ask them to recall the order of the colors of the animals.

2. Ask, "Who has visited a swamp? What did you see? How did you feel at the swamp? Would you want to explore a place that has wild animals in it? What should you do to make your visit safe?"
3. Use the animal patterns to make a coloring page for the children to take home.
4. Ask, "How are these animals alike?" (they all live in the swamp, they all eat fish and other food that also lives in the swamp, they are all alive, they are all wild, etc.). Then ask, "How are these animals different? (some eat big fish, some eat little fish, some are birds, some are reptiles, the raccoon is a mammal, some have feathers, some have scales, the pelican has a pocket, some fly, some swim, the turtle has a shell for a house, the raccoon has fur, etc.). Ask, "Which animal do you like best? Why?"

?

Why does a mother pelican lay eggs?
Because if she dropped them, they would break.

What makes more noise than a pelican stuck in a fishing net?
Two pelicans stuck in a fishing net.

Picture books about pelicans

*Indicates especially wonderful!

Ciardi, John, *The Reason For The Pelican*, 1959, J. B. Lippencott Co., Philadelphia, New York. This is the lead off poem of a volume of poetry of the same name. It's short and humorous and can be found on p. 9.

Freeman, Don, *Come Again, Pelican*, 1961, The Viking Press, New York, NY. Ty goes fishing, but despite his father's warnings, loses one of his new boots to the rising tide. His pelican friend has it in his pouch, so Ty rewards him by giving him the only fish that he caught that day.

Kent, Jack, *Joey Runs Away, 1985, Prentice Hall, Inc., Englewood Cliffs, NJ. Joey decides that it would be easier to run away from home than to clean his messy pocket. While he tries to move into a pelican and mail pouch, several animals try to move into his old room. Finally, he returns to clean his room. This story is also available on video and cassette tapes from Weston Woods, Weston, CT.

Lear, Edward,. (ill. Kevin W. Madison), *The Pelican Chorus & The Quangle Wangle's Hat*, 1981, The Viking Press, New York, NY. Colorful illustrations of pelicans accompany the Lear poem. The text may be appropriate for very small groups or slightly older children. No pockets, just pelicans.

****Ranger Rick***, a magazine published by the National Wildlife Federation, **March 1992, pages 3-6.** A full color spread of pelicans reciting humorous rhymes. The close-up detail in the photographs is excellent.

Roever, J. M., *The Brown Pelican*, 1974, Steck-Vaughn Co., Austin, TX. Line drawings illustrate facts relating to pelicans, particularly the endangered brown pelican. Some good drawings and references to the pelican's pouch.

Stone, Lynn, *The Pelican*, 1990, Dillon Press, Inc., Minneapolis, MN. Factual accounts of pelicans with full colored photographs on every page. Several photos of the pelican's pouch are included.

Wildsmith, Brian, *Pelican, 1982, Pantheon Books, a Division of Random House, Inc., New York, NY. Paul finds an unusual egg that turns out to be a pelican. After unsuccessful efforts to teach the bird how to fish, Paul's father insists that if the bird is to remain with the family, it must earn its keep. It carries groceries and lunches in its pocket beak. It finally learns to fish and leaves to join other pelicans.

Pelican Pouch Puppet

1. Enlarge and cut out the patterns. Cut one top head and two lower bills. Cut out the openings in both the lower bills. For best results, use poster board or cardboard.
2. To make a stretchy pouch, cut a piece of old nylon stocking slightly larger than the opening in the lower bill. Lay it over the opening without stretching it. Use masking tape to keep it in place. Then position the second lower bill over it and staple securely all around the opening so that the nylon will not pull out. Glue or tape around the outer edges to prevent separation.
3. Staple the doubled lower bill to the head and fold down along the dotted line. The mouth will open and close.

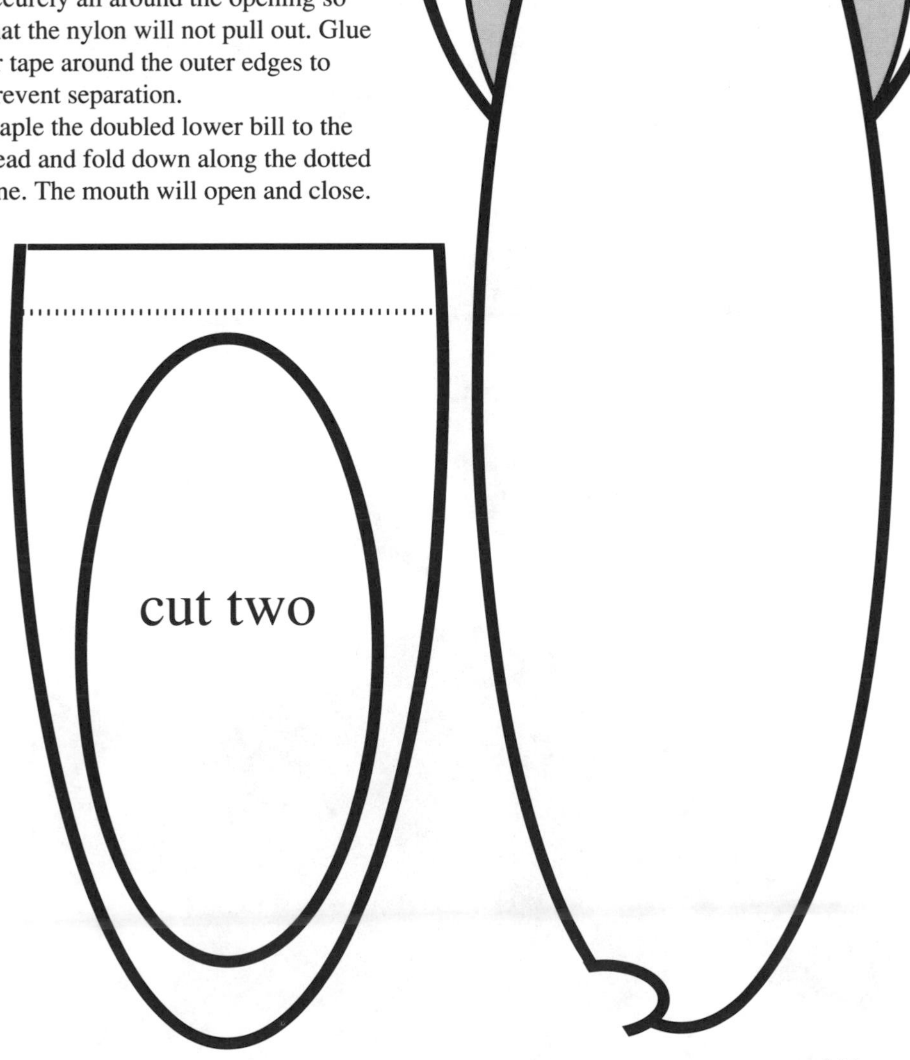

Egret: color
it white
Snake: color
the stripes
yellow.
Raccoon:
color it tan

Pelican: color the head
white and the body gray
Heron: color it blue
Turtle: color it green

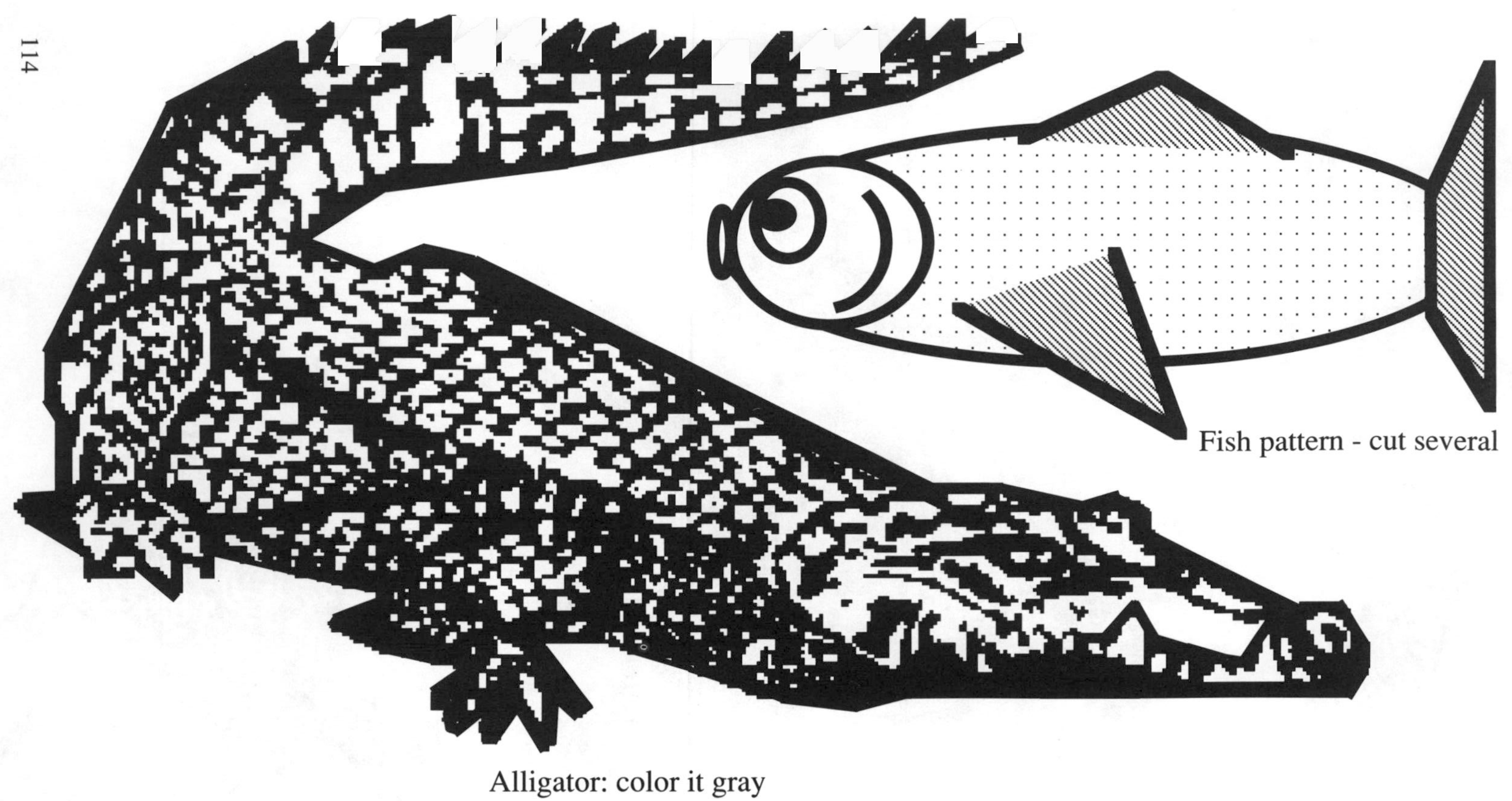
Fish pattern - cut several
Alligator: color it gray

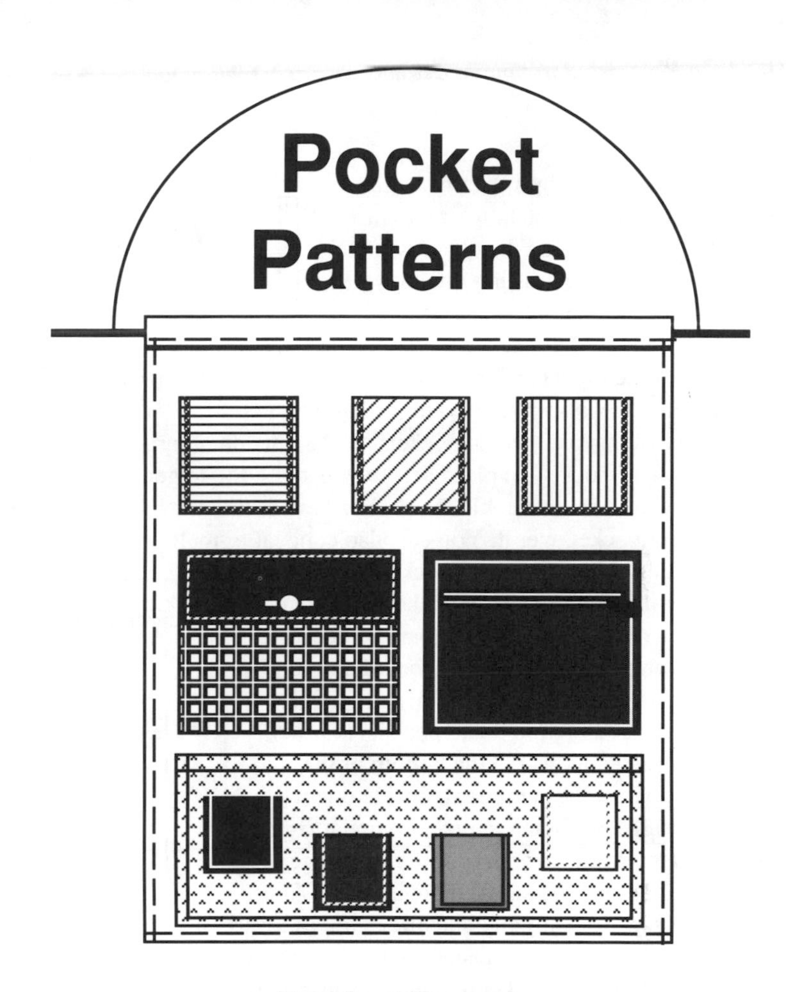

Pocket Board

This simple pocket board is a handy addition to any classroom or storytelling setting. It is perfect for many of the activities in this book, and can also be used to display seasonal artwork, store flannel board figures, storytelling props, and art supplies, or as a memo or communications board for classroom organization.

Start with sturdy, non-stretchy fabric with a tight weave (such as denim) for the base. Cut a rectangle of the fabric in the size to fit your needs, allowing an extra inch along all sides for a finished hem. Next add the number and arrangement of pockets that you need. The pocket board illustrated above has ten pockets. Eight are simple patch pockets (see p. 116), one is a zippered pocket (see p. 118), and one has a buttoned flap (see p. 119). But you can make as many different or same-sized pockets as your situation requires.

To make the hem, turn your base rectangle over so that the wrong side faces up. Fold over 1/2 inch along all sides, press, then fold over another 1/2

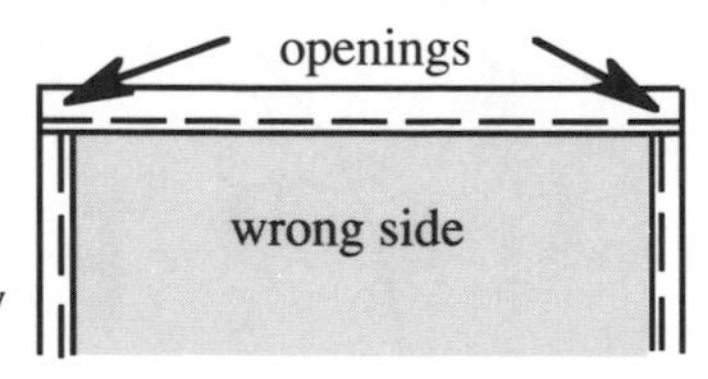

inch, so that all raw edges are finished. Stitch in place using matching or contrasting thread, depending on the effect you are trying to create. A contrasting thread, yellow with a navy-blue denim base for example, will create a blue jean look. Be sure to leave openings (see figure above) on both sides of the top where an optional 1/2 inch wooden dowel can be inserted and tied with string or yarn for hanging.

When placing small patch pockets on the outside of larger ones, be sure to sew the small pockets in place before you stitch the large pocket onto the base. If you want an inside, hidden pocket, sew it onto the base first, then put the larger pocket over it. You can also conceal a small pocket by sewing it to the wrong side of the large pocket.

cardboard base

For temporary purposes, a pocket board can be constructed from cardboard and posterboard. Cut the rectangular base from cardboard and the pockets from posterboard and simply staple into place. To strengthen, or to make pockets that will hold bulkier contents, staple the bottom of the pocket flat against the cardboard, upside down with the wrong side facing out (see figure at right) Then fold the pocket up and push the side edges slightly to the center before you staple them in place. The pocket will curve out slightly and allow you to insert bulkier items.

Place letters, numbers, shapes, animals, or other decorations or labels on the outside of each pocket to create a sorting/classification center. Fabric pockets can easily be labeled with permanent ink markers, but greater flexibility is created when labels are pinned or taped.

Patch Pockets

There are four types of patch pockets: fully lined, hemmed, cuffed, and untreated.

Fully Lined Patch Pockets

If hemming is aggravating to you, then you will like this technique, but it requires twice as much fabric as the other types. Instead of cutting one rectangle for your pocket, cut two of the identical size (they can be of different fabrics). Put right sides together, and sew a 5/8" seam all around, leaving a small opening for turning inside out. Turn it inside out, press, and it is finished. The opening will be stitched shut when you sew the pocket to a base. The lined pocket is very strong and no raveling will occur inside.

Hemmed Patch Pockets

Cut a rectangle 1 inch wider and 1 1/2 inches longer than you need for your finished pocket. With the wrong side facing up, press each raw edge up 1/2 inch. On the top side only, turn under another 1/2 inch, so that no raw edges will unravel at the opening. Sew the top hem in place. The side hems will be stitched when you sew the pocket in place. Raveling may occur inside, but this is not usually a big problem, especially if you have selected a fabric with a tight weave.

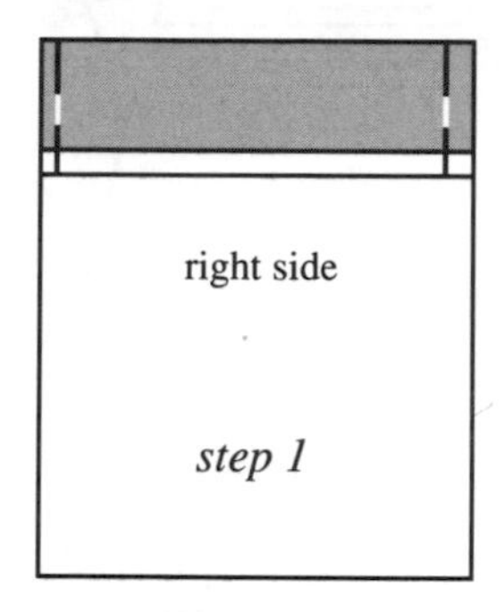

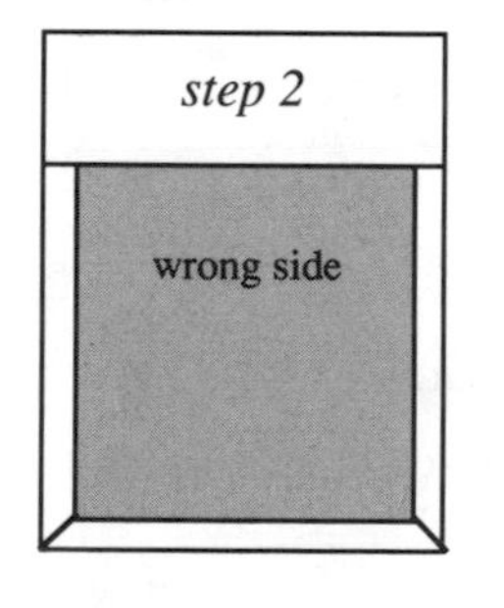

Cuffed Patch Pockets

This is a modified version of the hemmed pocket, used when you do not want the top hem stitching to show through, or when the pocket needs extra strength at the opening. Cut a rectangle 1 inch wider, and 2 1/2 inches longer than the finished pocket size that you need.

Fold over the top edge 2 1/2 inches, right sides together. Then press the raw edge up 1/2 inch. Stitch a 1/2 inch seam at the side edges of the rectangle as shown in *Step 1* at left.

Turn the cuff inside out. With the wrong side facing up, press the remaining raw edges in 1/2 inch to match the cuff, as shown in *step 2* at left. As with the hemmed pocket, the side edges will be stitched when the pocket is sewn in place.

Again, some raveling may occur, but this is a good choice for a pocket that will be stretched often by hands or bulky items.

Untreated Patch Pockets

This is the easiest and fastest pocket to make, but requires careful fabric selection. Simply cut the size pocket that you need, and sew it in place with no hemming or pressing. The fabric must be very tight and non-raveling, like flannel (beware of tearing) or bonded polyesters. Most polyester fabrics will roll, rather than ravel, but they also have a tendency to stretch, so if you use an unhemmed edge at the top, each time you insert something, that top edge will stretch out of place, resulting in a sagging pocket.

This problem can be partially eliminated by cutting the pocket against the grain. Find the grain by stretching the fabric in both ways. One way will be tight, the other stretchy. Cut the pocket so that the tight way forms the top edge. Looser weaves or raveling cottons can be used, but double or zig-zag stitching is necessary when sewing the pocket onto its base. If you are going to go to the trouble of double stitching, you may as well use a hemmed pocket - it's just as much work, but results in a superior product.

Untreated pockets may be glued, rather than stitched. The pocket found on the red hat on the front cover of this book was glued at the bottom and stitched along the sides. Because this pocket receives very little use and holds only light, flat objects, an untreated pocket was an appropriate option.

Zippered Pocket

Zippered pockets provide opportunities for practicing fine motor skills. To make a square pocket, cut a rectangle twice as long as it is wide (10" x 5" yields a 5" square).

Fold the rectangle as shown at right, with 1.5" on the top flap and 3.5" on the lower flap. Press the raw edges under 1/4 inch, and pin a closed 5" zipper between the flaps as shown. Stitch the zipper as close as possible to the edge of the fabric.

Open the zipper slightly, and turn the pocket inside out, so that the right sides are together and the wrong side is facing up. Stitch the side seams together as shown. Pull the right side of the pocket out through the opening in the zipper. Press and the pocket is complete.

Use the zippered pocket as a separate, portable pocket, or stitch it onto a base or apron.

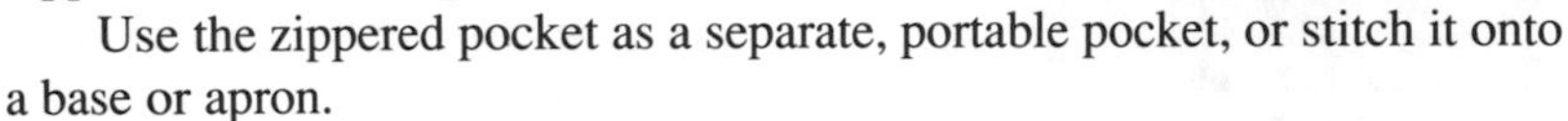

Belted Pocket

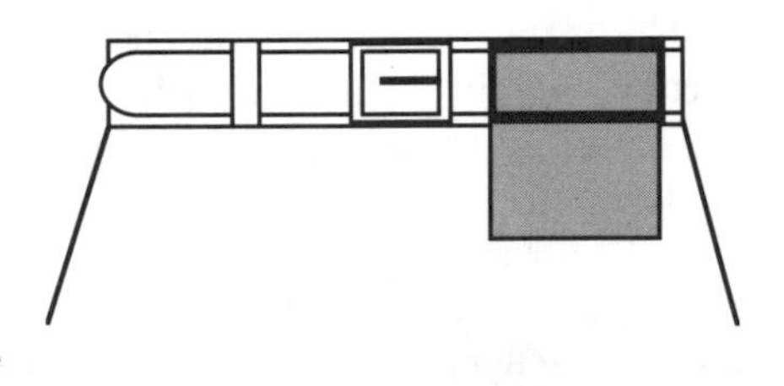

This pocket is easy to make and very practical to use. It slides on and off a belt and the flap can be fastened with a snap, Velcro, or a button.

Cut the pocket pieces according to the pattern on the top of the next page. To make the belted pocket, begin with the larger rectangle. Put right sides together and sew a 1/2" seam around all sides, leaving a small opening to pull the rights sides through. Turn it inside out, close the opening, and press.

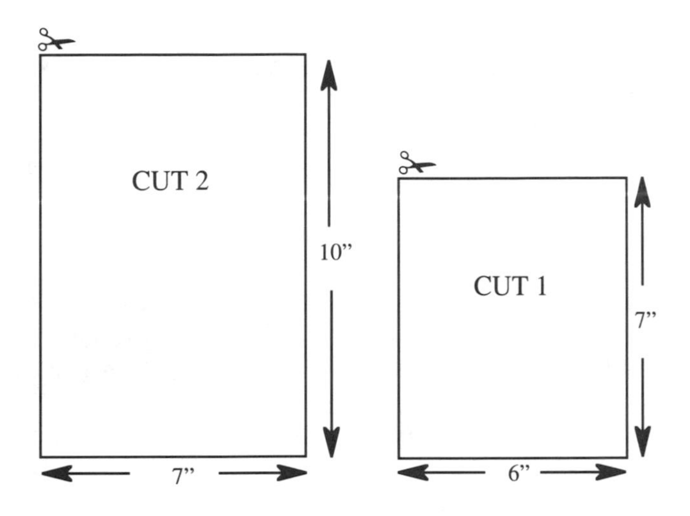

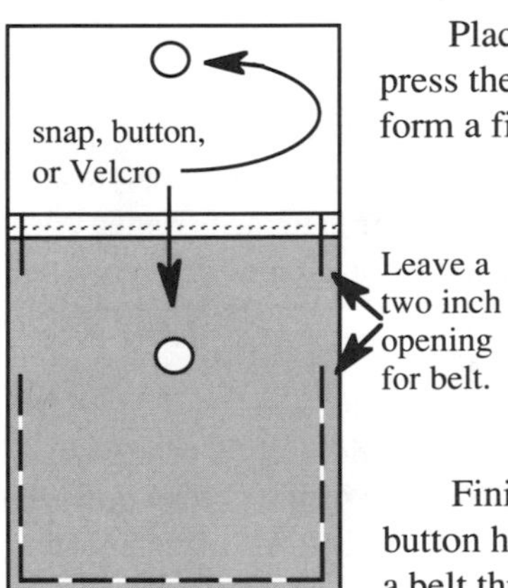

Place the smaller rectangle wrong side up and press the top edge up 1/2", and then another 1/2" to form a finished hem. Stitch in place.

Lay the right side of the smaller rectangle on the larger, lined piece. Stitch the top side edges together for one inch. Reinforce with double stitching. Then stitch around the rest of the pocket. Turn inside out and press the lined flap over the pocket.

Finish with snaps, Velcro, or a button (the button hole goes in the top lined flap section). Slip a belt through the pocket in the same way as you would with an ordinary belt loop.

Pocket With Buttoned Flaps

Follow the directions for the belted pocket pattern, except omit the opening for the belt. Stitch all around the pocket seam, turn inside out, and press the flap over the pocket. When sewing this pocket onto a base, be sure to open the flap and stitch only through the pocket portion, so that the flap remains free to open and close.

Make an excellent portable pocket by simply leaving it unattached.

Drawstring Pockets

Drawstring pockets were standard accessories for women until the 1830's when pockets finally began to be sewn into skirts, hence "Lucy Locket lost her pocket...." They were dangled from long ribbons attached to a woman's waist and accessible through a hidden slit in the skirt.

To make this pocket, cut a rectangle twice as wide as the finished pocket that you will need. Fold it in half and stitch 5/8" around the two open sides, as shown. Make a finished hem on top, leaving an opening in the seam (or cut a small hole) for the drawstring. Attach a safety pin to one end of the string, slip it through the opening, and work it around until it comes back out again.

Turn the pocket inside out, press, and tie the ends of the string together.

To make a rounded drawstring pocket, simply cut one circle and make a finished hem around the raw edges. As you sew the hem, occasional tucks will be necessary, as the outer edge is slightly longer than the hemmed edge. These tucks will not be noticeable when the drawstring gathers the pocket together.

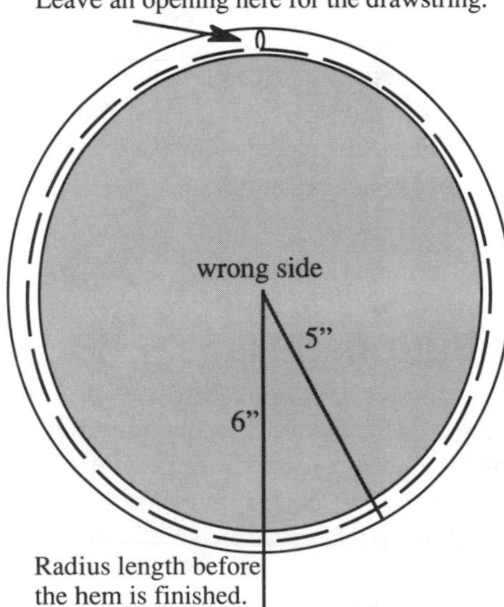

The radius of your circle (the length from the middle to the edge) will be the depth of your finished pocket. Allowing an inch for the hem all the way around, a circle that is 12" across will yield a finished pocket that is about 5" deep.

Ten Pocket Apron

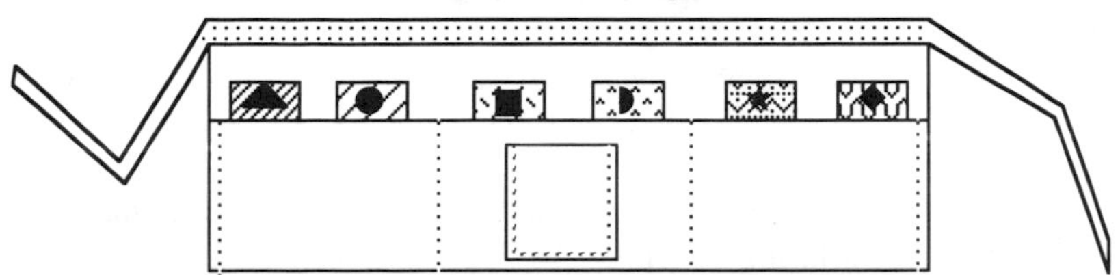

This apron can be worn by a person of any size and, like the pocket board, can be made using a variety of pocket sizes and types. The apron illustrated above has six hemmed patch pockets, one larger cuffed patch pocket in front, and three large pocket sections made by sewing dividing seams through a long strip of cloth. Here, the small patch pockets are labeled with different shapes, but could just as easily be labeled by numbers, vowels, names, colors, animals, or other classifications.

Begin by cutting out the pieces shown below. If you want zippered or buttoned pockets instead of patch pockets, simply substitute those according to the directions on previous pages. Decide what type of waistband you prefer. A strip of cloth 5" x 60" will provide an excellent waistband, but a thick grosgrain ribbon or wide cording drawn through the top will work just as well.

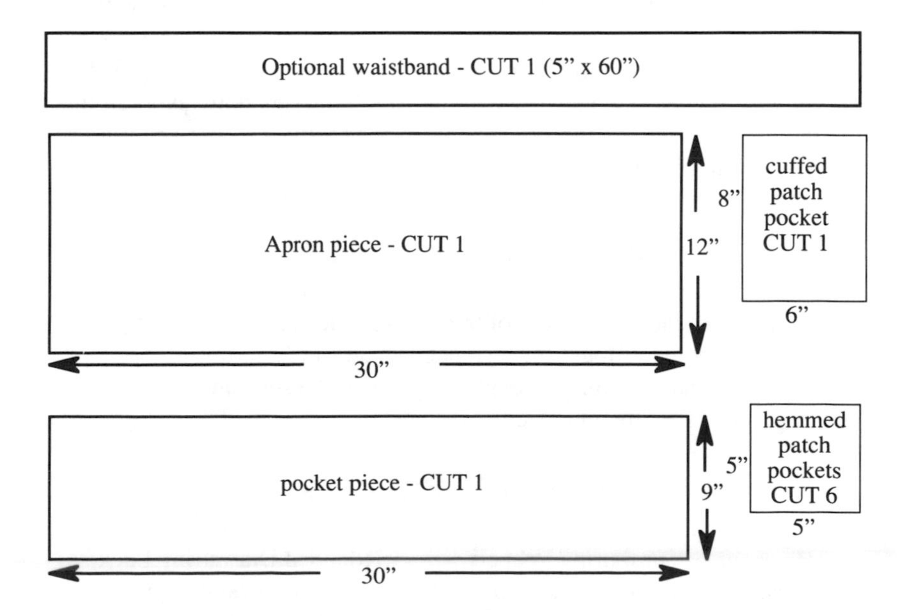

Begin sewing with the pocket piece. With the wrong side facing up, press 1/2" up along the top edge. Turn under another 1/2" to form a finished hem. Stitch in place.

Next, lay the apron piece down, with its *wrong side* facing up. Then align the bottom and lower sides with the pocket piece, also with its *wrong side* facing up. Stitch 5/8" along the bottom edge. Turn it inside out and press flat. The bottom of the pocket should be nicely stitched, with the *right sides* of both pieces facing up. Finish the side edges by turning under 1/2" twice through both thicknesses. Stitch in place.

Waistband Option: Cut a 5" x 60" strip from matching or contrasting fabric. Find the midpoint by folding in half vertically. Pin the midpoint of the waistband to the midpoint of the apron top, right sides together. Pin or baste along the rest of the apron top and stitch in place with a 5/8" seam.

Press the raw edge of the waistband under 1/2", fold it over, and pin it to the inside of the apron so that it slightly overlaps the stitching from the front. Stitch through all thicknesses, making sure that the stitching showing through on the front is on the waistband, not the apron. Finish off the remaining ties by pressing under 1/2" along all raw edges and sewing them together.

Drawstring Option: With the wrong side facing up, press the raw edge of the apron top up 1/2", then another inch. Stitch close to the edge, creating a slot 3/4" wide in which to insert the tie. Pull it through the slot so that the ties are the same length on both sides, then stitch in place or secure with a safety pin.

Sew extra pockets, labels, or decorations in place. Finish the apron by dividing the long pocket piece into thirds. Stitch through both layers from top to bottom. Reinforce the stitching at the top to give extra protection against pulling and tearing.

Recycled Jean Pockets

Cut a patch pocket off of old jeans, but be sure to cut out the pants underneath, too. Include enough of the pants fabric surrounding the pocket to allow for a border. Mount the jean pockets on sturdy cardboard or plywood. Attach by stapling through the pants of the surrounding border and/or gluing the entire underside of the pocket.

Portable Pockets

These pockets are ideal portable pockets when left unattached:

Rectangular Drawstring Pockets
Rounded Drawstring Pockets
Pockets With a Buttoned Flap
Zippered Pockets
Recycled Jean Pockets

Storytelling Aprons

Storytelling aprons are available in a variety of shapes and sizes from many teacher resource centers or suppliers. One of the best ones for use with young children is available from MJH Designs, 6722 Outer Lincoln, Newburgh, IN 47630, (812-853-3024). It is made from a very strong, washable fabric and has adjustable straps, so that one apron will fit all potential users. It has three pockets and functions like a portable flannel board. By attaching Velcro to props or characters, the storyteller can use her chest as a stage without ever having to turn away from her young audience. This apron comes with Velcro for attachments and is available in both adult and child sizes.

Storytelling aprons can be enhanced in unlimited ways by adding background scenery or props. See page 99 for sources that give instructions for how to use aprons in puppetry.

Commercial Pocket Charts

Many teacher resource centers or suppliers stock nylon charts that have clear acrylic slots or pockets lining one side. They are readily available and come in many different sizes, in both math and language arts departments. Special wall attachments and pocket chart stands are also offered. These can be easily adapted to many of the activities in this book, but the see-through characteristic of the plastic pocket slots eliminates the important motivators of curiosity and suspense. The slots could be made more mysterious by simply slipping a sheet of paper in front of the surprise you want your pocket to conceal.

Index for content areas and educational objectives

The author, Christine Petrell Kallevig, is available to present educational workshops or tell stories at conferences, conventions, festivals, or other gatherings. Contact the publisher, Storytime Ink International, P. O. Box 470505, Broadview Heights, Ohio 44147, for details.

If you liked the story, "Penny's Paper Pocket" on page 40, you are going to *love* these other paperfolding books by Christine Petrell Kallevig!

Folding Stories: Storytelling and Origami Together As One - Nine original short stories illustrated by nine easy origami models for ages preschool through adult. Includes extensive ideas for optional activities, complete illustrations and directions, photographs, glossary, and index. Recommended for storytellers, teachers, paperfolders, activity therapists or directors, and recreation leaders. ISBN 0-9628769-0-9 $11.50

Holiday Folding Stories: Storytelling and Origami Together For Holiday Fun - Nine original stories illustrated by nine easy origami models for ages preschool through adult, featuring historical facts and symbolism for Columbus Day, Halloween, Thanksgiving, Hanukkah, Christmas, Valentine's Day, Easter, May Day, and Mother's Day. Includes holiday facts, optional activities, complete instructions, illustrations, and photographs. ISBN 0-9628769-1-7. $11.50

Sunday Folding Stories: Old Testament Stories and Origami Together For Sunday School Fun - Favorite Old Testament stories retold and combined with easy origami models. Learn a new hobby through Bible stories. Includes complete illustrations, directions, photographs, and optional activities. Recommended for groups of all ages.
ISBN 0-9628769-4-1. $11.50

Use this coupon to order additional copies of **All About Pockets (ISBN 0-9628769-6-8 $9.95)** or any of the other popular books by Christine Petrell Kallevig. *(Library patrons: please photocopy.)*

name ______________________
address ______________________
____
city/state ______________________
zip code ______________________

Please send me:

Qty.	ISBN number	Price	Total
		SUBTOTAL	
		Ohio residents add 7% sales tax	
		Postage & handling: Add $2 (1st book), $1 @additional book	
		US dollars only TOTAL ENCLOSED	

Write checks to:
Storytime Ink International
Mail to:
Storytime Ink International
P. O. Box 470505
Broadview Heights, OH 44147-0505

Allow 4 - 6 weeks for delivery.